Rebekah's Confidence

Sharon Hoskins

ISBN: 978-0990824537

Scripture quotations were taken from the New King James Version
Copyright 1979, 1980, 1982, 1994 by Thomas Nelson, Inc.

CONTENTS

INTRODUCTION

Being confident in Christ comes as we grow in a relationship with the Father. In this study, we will dig into the life of Rebekah to find a confident woman, full of God's love, strong in her faith and obedient to all that He told her to do. Rebekah's relationship with God was seen in her everyday life as she served others, and she didn't look for anything in return. She displayed what the heart of a servant looked like on the outside because of the confidence in her Lord on the inside. There are many passages that can help us see into her life. She was introduced for the first time in Genesis Chapter 24 and we continue to read about her through Chapter 27.

Rebekah was chosen to be the wife of Isaac with whom God established His everlasting covenant. She was chosen to be the mother of two nations; Esau, the nation of Edom, and Jacob, the nation of Israel. She made some tough choices to stay in God's will and believed all that God promised her. She was tarnished with the reputation of being a deceiver because of her actions in getting Jacob the blessing that was meant for Esau. Her relationship with God gave her the confidence to live for Him no matter the cost, even if it meant her reputation.

This study will help show the evidence of a great woman who obeyed God and was confident in her relationship with Him; therefore, she accomplished what needed to be done for Him. She made a huge impact on the lives of her family members. She was a confident woman with the heart of a servant. She knew her God and she knew what He said for her to do. In this study we will look at eight points that bring out the heart of Rebekah and her confidence in the Lord. When God spoke to her, she believed Him and confidently moved at His command. She was a fascinating woman and we can learn from her if we will open our heart to hear. Each chapter of this book will reveal a different point that can strengthen our confidence as Christian women to live for Him at all costs.

The first point we find is the giving of the water, not only to the servant, but also to his ten camels. In this point, we will find how we can become a Camel Waterer for God, walking more in the spirit and less in the flesh.

The second point is the invitation to stay. She not only took in the servant, but his men and his camels. Here we will find how we can instill confidence into our children to live for God. They must have their own relationship with the Father and our prayers are very important for their lives.

The third point of Rebekah's confidence is her decision to go. In this section we will find how we can make the right decision for our lives in spite of what others think around us. Our family and friends may not understand decisions we make to follow God, so we must be confident in the choices we make for Him.

In the fourth point we will find Rebekah respectfully dismounting from her camel, covering herself, and bowing to her future husband. Being submissive has been

Rebekah's Confidence

misunderstood for many years and in this section an explanation will be given about how we can truly be submissive and not lose our identity. With a correct definition of submission, it will be easier for us to obey God in this area of our life.

In the fifth point we see that Rebekah went to the Lord. Here we will find how we also have the ability to hear from God. As our relationship with Him grows, then our confidence to hear Him will also grow.

The sixth point is that Rebekah believed the Lord. This shows us how we can not only go to God, but believe Him. We must be patient to wait on the Lord no matter how long it takes for the results to manifest.

The seventh point in this great woman's life is that she fulfilled the words of the Lord. This point will show us that we are responsible for being co-workers with God. In every relationship, we have a part to fulfill and our relationship with God is no different.

The eighth point of Rebekah's confidence is that she endured to the end. Everything God said was fulfilled; God did His part, Rebekah did her part and her life was successful for God. Her life wasn't perfect at all, there were things that she didn't like around her, situations that were difficult to endure, and people that made her life miserable, but her life was a success. She endured through the trials of her life and applied wisdom in making her decisions. Here we will learn how to obtain wisdom from our experiences in life and the knowledge we receive. The application of wisdom will help us endure to the end.

There is much to be said about a wise woman who learns from the trials of life, retains those teachings, and applies them in later situations to help her make better decisions. Our life is guided by our choices and decisions we make for ourselves. We can choose to follow God or our own emotions. We can make decisions based on God's word or based on how we feel. It is important as Christian women that we find confidence to live for God and endure to the end.

God gave us His written word along with the Holy Spirit to guide us in our life. He gave us stories like Rebekah and the Proverbs 31 Woman as examples for us to follow. Rebekah resembled the Proverbs 31 Woman and we can too when we understand what it truly means to be her. To be a woman that fears the Lord, that is kind, loving, content, giving, respectful, confident, and wise with the heart of a servant. With all these points we find a well-rounded woman that will teach us much about how we can be all that God has called us to be without losing our identity, our independence or our integrity and to rise up to be strong, wise, and confident women for God.

Chapter One

The story of Rebekah began in Genesis chapter twenty-four. In the beginning of this chapter Abraham has realized that he was getting old and before his death, he must make sure that Isaac will follow in the obedience of God. It was very important that Isaac did not marry any of the daughters of the Canaanites because intermarrying with the pagans would not be pleasing to the Lord. Purity of the bloodline is why they married within their own family during this time in history. Obtaining a wife from Abrahams own family would ensure that the bloodline stayed pure.

In Genesis 6:1-8 we have a scene that described why God destroyed the earth with the flood. His chosen people intermarried with pagans and caused the wickedness of man to be great upon the earth and the Lord with a grieved heart, became sorry that He had made man. This was why the bloodline was so important and Abraham had been instructed by God to keep it pure. Therefore, Abraham sent his oldest and most trusted servant to go to his country and his family to take a wife for Isaac from there. The servant swore an oath to Abraham that he would go to bring back a wife to Isaac but if she would not come with him, then he would be released from the oath. He would not, however, take Isaac back to the land from which he came. The servant started his journey in verse ten:

Genesis 24:10-21

"Then the servant took ten of his master's camels and departed, for all his master's goods were in his hand. And he arose and went to Mesopotamia to the city of Nahor. And he made his camels kneel down outside the city by a well of water at evening time, the time when women go out to draw water. The he said, "O Lord God of my master Abraham, please give me success this day, and show kindness to my master Abraham. Behold, here I stand by the well of water, and the daughters of the men of the city are coming out to draw water. Now let it be that the young woman to whom I say, 'Please let down your pitcher that I may drink,' and she says, 'Drink, and I will also give your camels a drink' – let her be the one You have appointed for Your servant Isaac. And by this I will know that You have shown kindness to my master."

And it happened, before he has finished speaking, that behold, Rebekah, who was born to Bethuel, son of Milcah, the wife of Nahor, Abraham's brother, came out with her pitcher on her shoulder. Now the young woman was very beautiful to behold, a virgin no man had known her. And she went down to the well, filled her pitcher, and came up. And the servant ran to meet her and said, "Please let me drink a little water from your pitcher." So she said, "Drink, my lord." Then she quickly let her pitcher down to her hand, and gave him a drink. And when she had finished giving him a drink, she said, "I will draw water for your camels also, until they have finished drinking." Then

Rebekah's Confidence

she quickly emptied her pitcher into the trough, ran back to the well to draw water, and drew for all his camels. And the man, wondering at her, remained silent so as to know whether the Lord had made his journey prosperous or not." (NKJV)

1. Giving of the Water

Rebekah was first introduced as a young woman at the community well in the evening time drawing water for the needs of her family. A physical description of her was given in verse sixteen. She was a young virgin and was very beautiful to behold. We will discover, however, that her beauty went much deeper than the physical. Just in the act of kindness in the scripture, we can see a glimpse into the beauty that lies deep in her heart through her actions.

Rebekah was not annoyed by the strangers need. She didn't make it a big deal when she was asked for a drink. Many of us would have done the same thing, it was just a drink. A drink for one man wouldn't have taken that long. Most of us would not, however, take on such a time consuming task of giving all of his camels some water. Rebekah went the extra mile which showed a Christ-like attitude as Matthew 5:41 states, *"And whoever compels you to go one mile, go with him two."* This was probably not the first time that Rebekah had watered camels or donkeys or some other animal. She displayed the characteristics of someone that was willing to do for others at a great sacrifice to herself.

We don't know how many trips she had made to the well or how far the well was, but we see in verse nineteen she said, *"I will draw water for your camels also, until they have finished drinking."* If we look at the evidence, we know that the servant had ten camels. Each camel can drink up to twenty-five gallons to replenish. Depending on her strength and the size of the pitcher, she could have made up to 83 trips. A gallon of water weighs 8.35 pounds. If she was able to carry three gallons (25 pounds) at a time, it would have taken nine trips to water one camel. It also would depend on how much water it took for each camel to be finished drinking. Even if she just made 10 trips that was still more than she was asked. No matter how many trips she made, she fulfilled her commitment.

We all have had someone make a commitment to us, but they never followed through. They started, but never finished. Promised, but never stood by it. Now think for a moment how many times you've promised something. Did you follow through with it? Rebekah willingly took on this man's burdens because she had a servant's heart. Galatians 6:2 says, *"Bear one another's burdens, and so fulfill the law of Christ."* Rebekah was so full of God that she looked like Him. Christ bore our burdens not for what we could do for Him, but to show His love for us. 1 John 4:10, *"In this is love, not that we loved God, but that He loved us and sent His Son to be the propitiation for our sins."* When we receive Jesus Christ as our Lord and Savior we start to look like Him in all that we say and do. It doesn't happen instantly or overnight, it is a journey that begins with receiving Christ. Then, as we learn and

Rebekah's Confidence

grow, we become more like Him. Rebekah did not become a camel waterer on this day, she was one. She already knew God and learned to listen to Him and that is exactly the kind of woman God needed for Isaac. Being a camel waterer meant that she had to deny herself, take up this burden and follow through.

This is the same attitude that is required of us to receive Christ. Matthew 16:24 says, *"If anyone desires to come after Me, let him deny himself, and take up his cross, and follow Me."* We deny ourselves when we repent of our sins, repent of the life we had been living and give it to Him. Our cross is the same burden that Christ bore which was and is people. We sacrifice our life so that others may know Christ. We follow Him in obedience to do all that He says to do. Rebekah denied herself, sacrificed her time, and obeyed, looking like Christ in her actions. This man was a stranger and she did not complain about anything. Philippians 2:14-16 says, *"Do all things without complaining and disputing that you may become blameless and harmless, children of God without fault in the midst of a crooked and perverse generation, among whom you shine as lights in the world, holding fast the word of life."*

She was able to do this because she had a relationship with the Father and it was seen in her actions; her fruit. *"The fruit of the Spirit is love, joy, peace, longsuffering, kindness, goodness, faithfulness, gentleness, self-control,"* Galatians 5:22-23 and with that comes humility. This is a great quality that is hard to obtain because the opposite of humility is pride and pride is sneaky. Pride takes many forms and creeps up when we are not looking. Rebekah was not prideful. If so, she would've said, "I am busy with my own thing, I don't have time for you, I have come all this way to the well for what my family needs, don't bother me." Pride speaks with body language, an attitude as well as words. Most often we will say something that sounds humble, but our attitude shows forth our pride. In Rebekah's case, her words and attitude were both that of humility and in humility, confidence shines. Pride is not a characteristic of confidence, but is in fact a characteristic of conceit. The dictionary describes conceit as:

1. Vanity – Full of ourselves – self-seeking interested in only what benefits us not anyone else.

2. Boasting – Sure of our own abilities – we'll only do what we know we can do as to not be embarrassed or shamed.

3. Prideful – Self-esteem – needing others to praise us for what we do; looking for recognition and a pat on the back.

None of these definitions describe Rebekah. She was humble and confident! She did not need a pat on the back or praise for her goodness. She was willing to be put to shame to serve someone in need. She was not looking for recognition in her giving. She simply did what was right because she was full of the fruit of the Spirit. She didn't say to the man, "here you can borrow my pitcher and get some water for the camels, it's been a long day for me

Rebekah's Confidence

and I have already been to the well once." She didn't say, "I feel for you and I know you have need but this is as far as I am willing to go." She was willing and confident enough within herself to be humble and give to someone else what they needed. In this case, the man needed water, his camels needed water and this required her time, energy, and humility. At this point, she had no idea that he was Abraham's servant. She had no idea he had just prayed to God for this specific sign. She also had no idea she would gain anything from this simple act of kindness.

Let's truly look into our hearts and ask ourselves, "What would we do in Rebekah's shoes?" Do we have the confidence to place ourselves in a servant's position? Do we place the needs of someone else before our own? Rebekah had gone to the well to get water for her family. Serving this stranger would delay her in her chores, but we see no evidence that she was upset by this delay at all. In fact, she offered more than he asked. Would you do this for others in your life? Are you annoyed to just do for your own husband or your children? When you do things for them, are you sure to let them know that you really didn't have time for it? Did you express that feeling of inconvenience by words or by attitude? We have all done this with someone in our life whether it is a boss, a spouse, a parent or a teacher. We do what we are told or asked, but not without giving our opinion with our attitude. This is a self-seeking attitude and it falls under the definition of conceit.

Confidence cannot be seen in a conceited person because they cannot live together in the same vessel. Confidence shows humility and conceit shows pride. We cannot be prideful and humble at the same time. We are either one or the other. Only through confidence and humility can we show the love of Christ to those around us. The love of Christ is obedience to the Father. What we learned from Rebekah in just this one section gives us a great understanding of her relationship with the Father, because He has these same characteristics.

She was a giving person. In her giving, there was a sacrifice. We see a sacrifice of her time and her energy. It was more important to her that his needs were met before her needs. This is the same attitude of our Father. He is a giving God and in His giving there was a sacrifice; Christ, so that we would have all we needed to be saved. John 3:17, *"For God did not send His Son into the world to condemn the world, but that the world through Him might be saved."* She gave more than what was asked of her. She saw the need, even though he didn't ask for it, and she did what she could to fulfill that need. This shows that she was attentive to the needs of others. God does this for us; He understands our needs and gives us more than we ask for. Ephesians 3:20-21, *"Now to Him who is able to do exceedingly abundantly above all that we ask or think, according to the power that works in us, to Him be glory in the church by Christ Jesus to all generations, forever and ever. Amen"* Her giving did not have a price. By not putting a price on her service she was given even more than she could have asked for. God does not put a price on what He gives to us. He gives a free gift and its value is more than all the money and things of this world; everlasting life. Romans 6:23 *"For the wages of sin is death, but the gift of God is eternal life in Christ*

Rebekah's Confidence

Jesus our Lord." Ephesians 2:8-9 *"For by grace you have been saved through faith, and that not of yourselves; it is the gift of God, not of works, lest anyone should boast."*

She sacrificed herself because she saw a need and she didn't require anything in return. Jesus said in John 15:13, *"Greater love has no one than this, than to lay down one's life for his friends."* When we give our life to Christ then our life should begin to change and our characteristics should start to imitate His. Ephesians 5:1-2 *"Therefore be imitators of God as dear children. And walk in love, as Christ also has loved us and given Himself for us, an offering and a sacrifice to God for a sweet-smelling aroma."* Paul writes in 1 Corinthians 11:1 *"Imitate me, just as I also imitate Christ."* These are all encouraging words to bring us to an understanding that all of us can be imitators of Christ if we will strive to.

Many of us strive to be good at something. Some people strive in their job to be the best at what they do. They follow all the rules and work extra hard. Some strive to be the best athlete. They workout, take vitamins, and refuse to let certain things cross their lips. They may be called negative things like brownnosers or health nuts, but they are striving to be the best. Some strive to be the best in school. They study and work hard to make the grade. Some strive to be the best moms. They do all they can to make sure their kids are involved and socialized. They might be called overachievers or soccer moms, but they are just striving to be the best.

If we would put as much effort into being the best for God and strive to imitate Him, then we could be the best at whatever God puts before us. What keeps us from striving to be Christ-like in our everyday living? John 12:42-43, *"Nevertheless even among the rulers many believed in Him, but because of the Pharisees they did not confess Him, lest they should be put out of the synagogue; for they loved the praise of men more than the praise of God."* Do you love the praise of men more than the praise of God? Who are the Pharisees in your life that keep you from confessing Him?

If you want to be all that God created you to be, then are you doing the foundation work to make it possible? This is where we get messed up, there is foundational work to be done before we step in and try to do things for God. We have to learn how to live in our new life as a new creation by sitting on the Potter's wheel and allowing God to show us changes we need to make in our own life. Be a disciple, which means learner, of God's truth before we can show others the Way. We do this by applying His teachings to our lives. As we do this, we will grow in confidence. So, when we give water to others in our lives, like Rebekah did to the stranger, we will be able to give in confidence just like her. In Mark 9:41, Jesus said, *"For whoever gives you a cup of water to drink in My name, because you belong to Christ, assuredly, I say to you, he will by no means lose his reward."*

In Matthew 25:40, Jesus tells His sheep because they have done for others, they have also done for Him. When we do for others only to gain something in return, we will usually be disappointed. However, if we give in confidence that we need nothing in return, the gift we get is priceless. Colossians 3:23-24 *"And whatever you do, do it heartily, as to the*

Lord and not to men, knowing that from the Lord you will receive the reward of the inheritance; for you serve the Lord Christ." Be honest and look at every part of our life; whether it is a wife, mother, daughter, friend, employee or co-worker and examine if we are showing the love of Christ to others. 2 Corinthians 13:5 says, *"Examine yourselves as to whether you are in the faith. Test yourselves."*

So, let's do some self-examination as we read Galatians 5:19-23. The first few verses speak of the flesh, our natural man. The last of these verses speak of the fruit that develops in us through the Holy Spirit. Can you recognize yourself in Gal 5:19-21? I would imagine that we all can identify with one or more of them at some point in our life. Maybe you are fighting one or more of them now. Look at these lists and examine your heart and see where repentance is needed.

Flesh

1. Adultery – unfaithfulness
2. Fornication – sexual immorality
3. Uncleanness – impurity of mind
4. Lewdness – obscene
5. Idolatry – anything that gets before God
6. Sorcery – witchcraft
7. Hatred
8. Contentions - strife
9. Jealousies
10. Outbursts of Wrath
11. Selfish Ambitions
12. Dissensions – causes division
13. Heresies – deny God's truths
14. Envy – to degrade others
15. Murders
16. Drunkenness
17. Revelries – stir up trouble

"…and the like; of which I tell you beforehand, just as I also told you in time past, that those who practice such things will not inherit the kingdom of God." Gal 5:19-21. Practice is the key word; we all may fall short at times in our life. Ask God to show you where you need to change, and then repent. God is faithful to cleanse you from all unrighteousness.

Rebekah's Confidence

Spirit

1. Love
2. Joy
3. Peace
4. Longsuffering
5. Kindness
6. Goodness
7. Faithfulness
8. Gentleness
9. Self-control

"...against such there is no law. And those who are Christ's have crucified the flesh with its passions and desires." Gal 5:22-24

Is your flesh crucified? _____. The first step to crucifying your flesh is to ask Jesus Christ to be your Lord and Savior. Ask Him to forgive you of your sins, turn from them and sin no more. If you have already taken this step, which parts of your flesh do you still need to crucify? _____

"If we live in the Spirit, let us also walk in the Spirit." Which parts of the Spirit do you have trouble walking in? Gal 5:25_____

"For he who sows to his flesh will of the flesh reap corruption, but he who sows to the Spirit will of the Spirit reap everlasting life." Examine your life. What you are sowing? Gal 6:4&8

_____

Ask God to reveal to you what areas of your flesh still need to be crucified. _____
_____

Ask God to strengthen you in the areas of the Spirit that you need help. _____
_____

As we look into God's Holy Word, it might hurt to see ourselves, but that's a good thing because then we will know how much we really need Jesus in every aspect of our lives. Jesus says, "These things I have spoken to you, that in Me you may have peace. In the world you will have tribulation; but be of good cheer, I have overcome the world." John 16:33.

Rebekah's Confidence

Chapter Two

Genesis 24:22-32

"So it was, when the camels had finished drinking, that the man took a golden nose ring weighing half a shekel, and two bracelets for her wrists weighing ten shekels of gold, and said, 'Whose daughter are you? Tell me, please, is there room in your father's house for us to lodge?' So she said to him, 'I am the daughter of Behuel, Milcah's son, whom she bore to Nahor.' Moreover she said to him, 'We have both straw and feed enough, and room to lodge.' Then the man bowed down his head and worshiped the Lord. And he said, 'Blessed be the Lord God of my master Abraham, who has not forsaken His mercy and truth toward my master. As for me being on the way, the Lord led me to the house of my master's brethren.'

So the young woman ran and told her mother's household these things. Now Rebekah had a brother whose name was Laban, and Laban ran out to the man by the well. So it came to pass, when he saw the nose ring, and the bracelets on his sister's wrists, and when he heard the words of his sister Rebekah, saying, 'Thus the man spoke to me,' that he went to the man. And there he stood by the camels at the well. And he said, 'Come in, O blessed of the Lord! Why do you stand outside? For I have prepared the house, and a place for the camels.' Then the man came to the house. And he unloaded the camels, and provided straw and feed for the camels and water to wash his feet and the feet of the men who were with him." (NKJV)

2. Invitation to Stay

From this passage we can now conclude that Rebekah continued to go back to the well until all the camels had finished drinking. She was not lacking in the commitment that she made with this man because she followed through to the end. Again, she denied herself, took up her cross, and followed Him, Matthew 16:24. Jesus also encouraged us to have this attitude about our Christian life when He spoke in Matthew 24:13, *"But he who endures to the end shall be saved."* Enduring till the end is in our daily living.

We must keep our commitments to each other and to God. If we speak without considering the sacrifice that we ourselves will have to pay, then we should still see it through no matter the cost. We must be careful that we don't volunteer for more than we can handle. If we speak too quickly and freely without thinking of the consequences, then we show a lack of integrity when we don't follow through. Then when we share Jesus, they think that He looks like us; uncommitted, untrustworthy and lacking integrity. He gets a bad name because we who claim to know Christ don't show the world what He looks like. Rebekah showed her integrity when she followed through with her commitment to water the camels

Rebekah's Confidence

until they finished drinking. She didn't give up half way through because they were drinking too much or because she was getting tired or because it was taking more time than she thought it would. She endured to the end and received a reward from God. Matthew 5:16 says, *"Let your light so shine before men, that they may see your good works and glorify your Father in heaven."* Where is our light to the world? Are the people around us seeing good works and glorifying God?

Rebekah showed forth her light by her works. She made the sacrifice and paid the price to do what she said she would. She let her yes be yes and her no be no as Jesus said in Matthew 5:37. She was a woman of integrity as well as confidence. Notice how she spoke to this man, this is who I am and we have food for your camels and room for you and your men to stay. She spoke to him in confidence. She did not feel that she needed to run home and ask her parents for permission before she made a decision to do something. We don't know how many men were with him, but we know he had ten camels. Feed for the camels alone would be a lot of giving, but she didn't hesitate to give it and more without getting permission from her family first.

She was confident that it was the right decision and was willing to endure the consequences if it was wrong. This brings us to an understanding about Rebekah's family and what they instilled in her. They taught her how to make decisions by letting her make them and then let her endure the consequences of them whether right or wrong. This act by her parents built her confidence. From that confidence she decided and agreed to give this man even more than she had already given. She just exerted herself to provide a drink for him and his camels, now he is asking for more. She did not gasp, "How dare he ask for more! I just gave him some water and ran back to the well several times to give his camels' water, and now he wants a place to stay with food to eat? If I give to him again, then what more will he ask for?" (Funny, she is next on the list.) But, without hesitation, she gave more before she had any idea why he was there. She didn't know that he had prayed and was on a mission from God for her. She had received a gift from him, but she didn't care if she received anything from him. She just did what was right because she walked in the fruit of the Spirit. Her actions showed a Christ-like attitude, Matthew 25:35 says, *"For I was hungry and you gave Me food; I was thirsty and you gave Me drink I was a stranger and you took Me in."* When we do for others, we do for God. In her confidence, Rebekah did just that.

She was confident in her giving. She didn't spit and sputter and think about what this invitation may cost her or her family. The food for these men and the camels was no doubt costly for this family. Not just the financial aspect of it, but what it cost them individually. The biggest cost we see here is the time that was put into these guests. Rebekah gave much of her time at the well. Her brother put much of his time in preparing the house and a place for the camels. Time was given preparing water for washing and food for eating. Time was a hard thing to give then and still is because we really have so little of it. We don't eat right because we don't have time to cook and we're out of shape because we don't have time to exercise. We let someone else clean our house, walk our dog, raise our children because

9

Rebekah's Confidence

we don't have time. Time is a precious commodity that we are willing to pay big for and the cost is more than dollars and cents. We pay with our health, our relationship with our children, and working together as a family.

Society has put job descriptions on family duties. Women are to clean house, cook meals, and tend to children. Men are to mow the lawn, fix the door, and take out the trash. What if we all came together as a family and helped each other no matter the gender? What an amazing concept. There may be less fighting between family members because one person would not feel as if they were working alone or expected to do something because it was their "job". Children would learn to work with their parents as a team in the family unit. Maybe our children would have more appreciation if they had to work. This family worked together and did not let the lack of time stop them from giving food, water, and shelter to a group of strangers and their livestock. This act of kindness shown by this family is evidence that they walked in the Spirit; we recognize the fruit. They also taught Rebekah to walk in the Spirit. When no one else was there to tell her what to do she did what was right. Proverbs 22:6 says, *"Train up a child in the way he should go, and when he is old he will not depart from it."* This family trained Rebekah up in the Spirit of God; we see the evidence because of who she was.

In every relationship we have a role to play and that role varies with each relationship. One of the most important roles we play is as mothers to our children. They are little individuals that we should be training to live in this world. Many Christians have made the decision to remove their children from the world. Jesus taught His disciples differently. He taught them to live in the world. In John 17:11-19, Jesus prays for them saying,

> *"...Holy Father, keep through Your name those whom You have given Me, that they may be one as We are. While I was with them in the world, I kept them in Your name. Those whom You gave Me I have kept; and none of them is lost expect the son of perdition, that the Scripture might be fulfilled. But now I come to You, and these things I speak in the world, that they may have My joy fulfilled in themselves. I have given them Your word; and the world has hated them because they are not of the world, just as I am not of the world. I do not pray that You should take them out of the world, but that You should keep them from the evil one. They are not of the world, just as I am not of the world. Sanctify them by Your truth. Your word is truth. As You sent Me into the world, I also have sent them into the world. And for their sakes I sanctify Myself, that they also may be sanctified by the truth."*

We need to teach our children how to live in the world. If we remove them from the world, they will not understand the world when they are forced to live in it. They won't know how to make decisions on their own. We want so badly for our children to succeed and make right choices that we are guilty of stepping in and making decisions for them. We have also been guilty of not making them endure the consequences of any bad decisions because we don't want to punish them for making a mistake. Both of these actions can hinder our children from being confident adults for Christ!

Many of us did not obtain confidence from our parents or our peers but we can make a difference in our children's lives and the lives of the children in our communities; by being confident ourselves. So how do we now gain confidence in ourselves? After so many years of low esteem and degrading thoughts how can we pull ourselves out and become confident? Hebrews 10:24-25 says, *"And let us consider one another in order to stir up love and good works, not forsaking the assembling of ourselves together, as is the manner of some, but exhorting one another, and so much the more as you see the Day approaching."*

We must help each other by stirring up love and by exhorting each other. Romans 12:9-13 says, *"Let love be without hypocrisy. Abhor what is evil. Cling to what is good. Be kindly affectionate to one another with brotherly love, in honor giving preference to one another; not lagging in diligence, fervent in spirit, serving the Lord; rejoicing in hope, patient in tribulation, continuing steadfastly in prayer; distributing to the needs of the saints, given to hospitality."* We must find the good in each other and seek to show love, kindness, and patience so we can honor each other. Rebekah's parents nurtured her to confidence. She said to the servant, "I am", and we need to be able to say, "I am", even if we have to nurture ourselves to that confidence. Just remember the difference between confidence and conceit; they are easily confused. We must learn to be confident in who we are in Christ so we can nurture others to confidence.

We may not be as fortunate as Rebekah, but we can do better for our children and for ourselves because of our relationship with Christ. The closer we walk with Him, the closer He walks with us. *"Draw near to God and He will draw near to you. Cleanse your hands, you sinners; and purify your hearts, you double-minded"* James 4:8. We get as much of God as we ask for. *"Ask and it will be given to you; seek and you will find; knock and it will be opened to you. For everyone who asks receives, and he who seeks finds, and to him who knocks it will be opened"* Matthew 7:7-8.

Many people have interpreted this to mean worldly possessions, but God is talking about the needs in our lives. What more do we need than Him? Satan is the only one that promises worldly things. In Matthew 4:8-9, *"Again, the devil took Him up on an exceedingly high mountain, and showed Him all the kingdoms of the world and their glory. And he said to Him, All these things I will give You if You will fall down and worship me."* We don't see God promising anything of this world. In fact, He warns against it. *"Do not lay up for yourselves treasures on earth, where moth and rust destroy and where thieves break in and steal; but lay up for yourselves treasures in heaven, where neither moth not rust destroys and where thieves do not break in and steal"* Matthew 6:19-20.

Jesus tells the rich young ruler in Matthew 19:21, *"If you want to be perfect, go, sell what you have and give to the poor, and you will have treasure in heaven; and come follow Me."* What are the treasures of heaven that Jesus is talking about here?

Rebekah's Confidence

"But those who desire to be rich fall into temptation and a snare, and into many foolish and harmful lusts which drown men in destruction and perdition. For the love of money is a root of all kinds of evil, for which some have strayed from the faith in their greediness, and pierced themselves through with many sorrows. But you, O man of God, flee these things and pursue righteousness, godliness, faith, love, patience, gentleness. Fight the good fight of faith, lay hold on eternal life, to which you were also called and have confessed the good confession in the presence of many witnesses. I urge you in the sight of God who gives life to all things, and before Christ Jesus who witnessed the good confession before Pontius Pilate, that you keep this commandment without spot, blameless until our Lord Jesus Christ's appearing, which He will manifest in His own time, He who is the blessed and only Sovereign, the King of kings and Lord of lords, who alone has immortality, dwelling in unapproachable light, whom no man has seen or can see, to whom be honor and everlasting power. Amen. Command those who are rich in this present age not to be haughty, nor to trust in uncertain riches but in the living God, who gives us richly all things to enjoy. Let them do good, that they be rich in good works, ready to give, willing to share, storing up for themselves a good foundation for the time to come, that they may lay hold on eternal life" 1 Timothy 6:9-19.

If we look at these Scriptures, we see Rebekah described. Even though we see the wealth of her family, she was not haughty. We see that she pursued righteousness, godliness, faith, love, patience, and gentleness. She was rich in good works, was ready to give, willing to share, and she stored up for herself a good foundation. That foundation for us should be in Jesus Christ, the Rock. *"Therefore whoever hears these sayings of Mine, and does them, I will liken him to a wise man who built his house on the rock: and the rain descended, the floods came, and the winds blew and beat on that house; and it did not fall, for it was founded on the rock"* Matthew 7:24-25. When we build our life on Christ, the Rock, we can stand firm on our foundation in confidence. Then we will also be rich in good works ready to give and willing to share.

All of us are busy and we sometimes feel that we can't do much for God, but if we all work together, we could help many know God. Rebekah didn't go home and have to do all the preparing alone. Her entire family pitched in to make these men welcome. The food, the water for washing, the place for the camels, and everything else that needed to be done was accomplished together as they worked unified for one purpose. This is what God expects of us. *"For as the body is one and has many members of that one body, being many, are one body, so also is Christ."* 1 Corinthians 12:12. Then, verse 27 says, *"Now you are the body of Christ, and members individually."* Ephesians 4:15-16 *"But, speaking the truth in love, may grow up in all things into Him who is the head – Christ – from whom the whole body, joined and knit together by what every joint supplies, according to the effective working by which every part does its share, causes growth of the body for the edifying of itself in love."*

We should all be doing our share to cause growth in the body of Christ. It didn't matter to Rebekah's family who invited these men to stay. They didn't make it her job to see that

Rebekah's Confidence

these men had what was needed; they jumped in to help do wherever they could. The body of Christ should work this same way. Jumping in to help wherever needed, in prayer and devotion to each other. This attitude of Rebekah's family shows us much about how she was raised, about what was instilled in her and how the relationship that she had with her parents gave her confidence to be all that God created her to be.

It is important that we take this concept of unity and not only apply it to our family unit but also to our church family unit. We need to become unified for the purpose of the kingdom of God, to glorify the Father and let our light shine before others. Many people don't have unity in their homes so the division at church seems natural. In looking at God's word, however, it can be seen that He intends for us to be unified as we are called a body of Christ. *"But above all these things put on love, which is the bond of perfection and let the peace of God rule your hearts, to which also you were called in one body; and be thankful"* Colossians 3:14-15.

We were called in one body and we should work together for the same cause giving to each other as unto the Lord. *"And whatever you do in word or deed, do all in the name of the Lord Jesus, giving thanks to God the Father through Him"* Colossians 3:17. Also Colossians 3:23-24 says, *"And whatever you do, do it heartily, as to the Lord and not to men, knowing that from the Lord you will receive the reward of the inheritance; for you serve the Lord Christ."* It seems we would rather compete with each other and get some credit from men than give to each other and get our reward from God. Why is this so common in our lives today? Do we also do this with our families? Are we competing with our spouse or completing them? Are we competing with our children or complimenting them?

Encouragement and uplifting words go a long way to strengthen others, but it must start in our homes. We should not point out our husband's faults, but encourage his strengths. When disciplining, we should not tell our children that they are not good, but that their actions weren't good. It is so easy for the two to get confused and before we know it, they think they are stupid, bad, and not good for anything. They become followers of the kids at school because they think those kids are better than they are. In their effort to be better, they lose their own identity.

Much was learned from this section about supporting our children and each other to encourage them to be all that God created them to be, but it starts with us. Now that we have heard, what will we do? It is the doers that are successful; not the hearers only. James 1:25 says that a doer of the word will be blessed in what he does. We have to do something to make a difference in our own lives first, and then we will be able to help others.

What one positive thing can you say about yourself? _____
_____
_____
_____

Rebekah's Confidence

Satan has done a great job in making us women feel helpless, useless, weak, unworthy, and invaluable. He has put people in our paths of life to tell us these things, he has put negative thoughts in our mind about ourselves, and he has created situations around us to back up the rest. He has been very convincing and we have believed him. When people sling negative words, we grab them and keep them as our own. We are so willing to take the negative things others say about us and magnify them. Then we try to hide that negative person we think we are. This causes us to become prideful, conceited, and vain. The reason this happens is because we are trying to convince others that we are not the negative person we believe we are. However, if we were just honest, the real person could be seen but the real person is hidden behind falseness. This is a cloak that hides our heart not only from others, but also from God. That is exactly what Satan wants to do. He wants to keep us from seeing the truth about who God says we are, so he keeps us believing what others are saying.

So then, when we are given a compliment, we brush it off, "It's just God," we say. That is false humility. If we are all Christians, then the Holy Spirit lives in us. We are all different and have different abilities. *"But now God has set the members, each one of them, in the body just as He pleased. And if they were all one member, where would the body be?"* 1 Corinthians 12:18-19. The truth is that it is easier to believe the negative things and reject the things which are true and praiseworthy. We think that if we say or believe anything positive about ourselves that we are being prideful or conceited. *"I have been crucified with Christ; it is no longer I who live but Christ lives in me; and the life which I now live in the flesh I live by faith in the Son of God, who loved me and gave Himself for me"* Galatians 2:20. So, if our flesh, which is conceited, is crucified then our Spirit, which is confident, will be strengthened. We will no longer be trying to prove to others that we are useful, strong, and valuable. We will just be confident that we are all of those things in Christ. That is why Philippians 4:8 says, *"Whatever things are true, whatever things are noble, whatever things are just, whatever things are pure, whatever things are lovely, whatever things are of good report, if there is any virtue and if there is anything praiseworthy – meditate on these things."* When we meditate on the positive things then Satan can't use our faults against us. So, if we have given our life to Christ, then we should continue to surrender more and more of our heart to Him. In return, He will strengthen our confidence because our confidence comes from Christ when he lives in us.

Ask God to show you where you lack confidence. _____

_____

_____

_____

_____

_____

Realizing that we can change no one, but God can change us, answer these questions looking only at you.

Rebekah's Confidence

1. In your family, is there competition with your spouse or children? _____

2. How can you change the competitive attitude that is against each other, to a completing attitude that is unified? _____

_____

_____

_____

3. Does your church family compete with each other? _____

4. What could you do to change the competitive attitude that is against each other, to a completing attitude that is unified? _____

_____

_____

_____

_____

_____

5. What things did you see with Rebekah in this section that inspired you in your walk with God? _____

_____

_____

_____

_____

_____

_____

_____

6. Write your name in the blank.

Look in the mirror every morning and say:

My name is _____.

I am loved by God. He created me in my mother's womb. He has blessed me with every spiritual blessing in the heavenly places in Christ, He chose me, adopted me, and redeemed me by His blood. I can trust Him; He works all things together for my good and His glory so I can do all things through Christ who strengthens me.

This will build your confidence in Christ.

Now, as for our children, we all want the best for them so we can pray for them just as Jesus prayed for His disciples. *"Holy Father, keep through Your name those whom You have given Me, that they may be one as We are"* John 17:11. We all believe that our children are given to us by God and we want them to know Christ as we do.

Rebekah's Confidence

7. Fill in the blanks to personalize your prayer to God for you and your children/child. Using their name(s), him/her/them, he/she/they or his/her/their where appropriate.

Holy Father, keep through Your name, _____, my children/ child whom You have given me. Help me teach _____ how to be one with You. While I have _____ with me, help me to keep _____ in Your name. Guide _____ in Your will that _____ may fulfill all that You have for _____ to do. Fill me with Your joy that I may give it to _____. Help me to nurture _____ to confidence that _____ may not be swayed by _____ peers to walk against You. Give _____ wisdom to walk in the world without being part of it. I ask Father that You keep _____ from the evil one. Sanctify me that I may be an example before _____ and _____ would desire to be sanctified also. Help me be a light in _____ life. I love You Lord and thank You for all You have given me. In Jesus name I pray....Amen.

This will build their confidence in Christ

Rebekah's Confidence

Chapter Three

Genesis 24:33-58

Food was set before him to eat, but he said, "I will not eat until I have told about my errand." And he said, "Speak on." So he said, "I am Abraham's servant. The Lord has blessed my master greatly, and he has become great; and He has given him flocks and herds, silver and gold, male and female servants, and camels and donkeys. And Sarah my master's wife bore a son to my master when she was old; and to him he has given all that he has. Now my master made me swear, saying, 'You shall not take a wife for my son from the daughters of the Canaanites, in whose land I dwell; but you shall go to my father's house and to my family, and take a wife for my son.'

And I said to my master, 'Perhaps the woman will not follow me.' But he said to me, 'The Lord before whom I walk, will send His angel with you and prosper your way; and you shall take a wife for my son from my family and from my father's house. You will be clear from this oath when you arrive among my family; for if they will not give her to you, then you will be released from my oath.'

And this day I came to the well and said, 'O Lord God of my master Abraham, if You will now prosper the way in which I go, behold, I stand by the well of water; and it shall come to pass that when the virgin comes out to draw water, and I say to her, 'Please give me a little water from your pitcher to drink,' and she says to me, 'Drink, and I will draw for your camels also,' let her be the woman whom the Lord has appointed for my master's son.' But before I had finished speaking in my heart, there was Rebekah, coming out with her pitcher on her shoulder; and she went down to the well and drew water.

And I said to her, 'Please let me drink.' And she made haste and let her pitcher down from her shoulder, and said, 'Drink, and I will give your camels a drink also.' So I drank, and she gave the camels a drink also. Then I asked her, and said, 'Whose daughter are you?' and she said, 'The daughter of Bethuel, Nahor's son, whom Milcah bore to him.' So I put the nose ring on her nose and the bracelets on her wrists. And I bowed my head and worshiped the Lord, and blessed the Lord God of my master Abraham, who has led me in the way of truth to take the daughter of my master's brother for his son. Now if you will deal kindly and truly with my master, tell me. And if not, tell me, that I may turn to the right hand or to the left."

Then Laban and Bethuel answered and said, "The thing comes from the Lord; we cannot speak to you either bad or good. Here is Rebekah before you; take her and go, and let her be your master's son's wife, as the Lord has spoken." And it came to pass, when Abraham's servant heard their words, that he worshiped the Lord, bowing himself to the earth. Then the servant brought out jewelry of silver, jewelry of gold, and clothing, and gave them to Rebekah. He also gave precious things to her brother and to her mother. And he and the men who were with him ate and drank and stayed all night.

Then they arose in the morning, and he said, "Send me away to my master." But her brother and her mother said, "Let the young woman stay with us a few days, at least ten; after that she may go." And he said to them, "Do not hinder me, since the Lord has prospered my way; send me away so that I may go to my master." So they said, "We will call the young woman and ask her personally." Then they called Rebekah and said to her, "Will you go with this man?" And she said, "I will go." (NKJV)

3. Decision to Go

In this scene the servant has told his purpose, gave more gifts, ate, drank, and stayed the night. When morning came, he was ready to leave, but opposition steps in the way. Everything was fine the night before during the celebration, but when it came time to watch Rebekah walk out the door, the fun had ended. However, Rebekah made the decision to go. She agreed right here at this moment to be Isaac's wife even though she had never met him. This practice of marriage was common in this time. Women usually didn't have a choice. They were given, betrothed or taken as wives. This was exactly what happened to Rebekah. Her brother and her father had given her the night before, but when it came right down to actually letting her go, the mother and brother wanted more time.

When Rebekah was given a choice, she chose to go even when her family wanted her to stay. She was showing her belief that this was God's plan for her life by standing against her family. She based her decision on information. The servant told the story of how he came to the well, prayed to the Father, and how she fulfilled that prayer. She witnessed his worship to the Lord; how he bowed himself to the earth, the way he spoke to God and the sincerity of his heart. She witnessed his determination when he chose not to eat until he had told his story to make sure that they were informed about why he was really there. All of that combined with what she knew to be true in her own heart gave her the confidence to make this decision.

The follow-through of this decision was not easy. She did not have the support of her family. They did not want her to go probably for different selfish reasons. We can all understand how it feels to be pressured by others, but Rebekah didn't let anything sway her from what she knew to be the truth. This again shows her walk with God as Matthew 10:37 says, *"He who loves father or mother more than Me is not worthy of Me. And he who loves son or daughter more than Me is not worthy of Me."* She desired to be in God's plan and was confident that it was His plan for her to go.

It is clear to see that God's plan cost her time with her family. She had to move away from her mother, father, and brother. She had to move away from the only place she had

Rebekah's Confidence

ever known. The journey to Isaac was roughly 450 miles so it was possible that she would never see her family again. It took confidence to make the decision to go and to pay the price. But, she had perfect confidence because she knew that she was following in God's plan for her life. So, we should know that when God calls, there is always a price to pay and that it is always worth the price to be in God's perfect plan.

Did you know that you can be in God's plan and not know it? This is where we may get a little confused at times. You may think that because you have not surrendered to some specific ministry that you are not in God's plan, but being in a specific ministry doesn't automatically make you in God's plan. It is very easy to confuse service with purpose. God's plan for you right now may be for you to sit quietly, listen, and learn about Him. *"So then, my beloved brethren, let every man be swift to hear, slow to speak, slow to wrath; for the wrath of man does not produce the righteousness of God"* James 1:19-20.

God lets us go through things that are sometimes unpleasant, and difficult. This doesn't mean we have stepped out of God's plan. When hard times come our way it builds character, creates experiences and gives us compassion. *"We also glory in tribulations, knowing that tribulation produces perseverance; and perseverance, character; and character, hope"* Romans 5:3-5. These difficult times draws us nearer to God as we seek Him through the adversity. It can be tempting to try to fix things on our own, to try to make things happen or keep some things from happening, but when we give it all to Him, He will see us through in miraculous ways. So, the important thing is to trust Him as we are going through these things, making decisions each day to do things His way, at His time, and on His terms. This will place us and keep us in His perfect plan for our life.

Rebekah's family wanted to take control of the situation, agreeing to obey God but by their own terms. Genesis 24:55 states, her mother and brother wanted ten more days with her, so it was agreed that she would go, but they wanted to be in control of the going. However, Rebekah refused to be out of line with God. She didn't let the hurt stop her from going which took confidence. This was exactly what God wanted her to do. Remember what she had witnessed with the servant; the testimony that he gave her family along with the role she played at the well. This in itself may have been the deciding factor that kept her confident in the decision to go. She knew that God had sent this servant on a mission for Isaac, and believed that she had been hand selected by God to be his bride. What a great honor; that God would think so highly of her that He would give her the privilege to be the mother of His chosen people.

In our Christian walk we are sometimes guilty of doing what Rebekah's family did. We surrender to do a job for God, but then we forget that He is the boss. We take control of when, where, and how we do things and expect God to bless our work. This will quickly remove us from His plan and God does have a great plan for all of us. There are no small jobs with God. Everything we do for God is important. Everything He asks us to do has a purpose. 1 Corinthians 12 says, *"There are diversities of gifts, but the same Spirit. There are differences of ministries, but the same Lord. And there are diversities of activities, but it is the same God who works all in all."* God distributes to each one individually as He wills. The body is made up of many members, not just one. *If the whole body were an eye, where would be the hearing? If the whole were hearing, where would be the smelling?* But now God has set the members, each one of them, in the body just as He pleased.

Pleasing God should be our focus, not which member He has created us to be. What does it matter whether you are an eye, ear, foot or hand? If you are a useful member, shouldn't that be enough? Who are we to reply against God? Are we not to be clay in the Potter's hands? As Romans 9:20-21 says, *"But indeed, O man, who are you to reply against God? Will the thing formed say to him who formed it, 'Why have you made me like this?' Does not the potter have power over the clay, from the same lump to make one vessel for honor and another for dishonor?"* Will we be satisfied with what God asks of us? If we are found faithful over few things, He will make us ruler over many things.

In the parable of the talents three servants were given just what they could handle. One was given five talents another given two talents and the other was given one talent. The servant with five talents and the servant with two talents doubled their talents for the master. To them he said, *"Well done, good and faithful servant; you were faithful over a few things, I will make you ruler over many things. Enter into the joy of your lord."* (Matthew 25:21&23) Sadly, the servant given one talent hid it and was not faithful to use it for the Lord's glory. The scriptures say that he was afraid so we can't allow fear to rob us of following the Lord even when the price seems too high to pay. Then, there are other times when we take on more than we can handle. Instead of taking what God gives us and using it for His glory, we have our eyes on what someone else has. With our eyes on others talents we don't appreciate and work within the talents He has given us.

Often, we are blind to these child-like behaviors that keep us in bondage to fear. We all know that when a baby is born they have to learn to use their eyes; they learn sounds, and how to talk. They learn to crawl before they walk. We accept this about babies in the physical, but for some reason, we don't want to accept this with our new Christian walk. Jesus tells Nicodemus in John 3:3, *"Most assuredly, I say to you, unless one is born again, he cannot see the kingdom of God."* Being born again or anew, as the Greek defines it, gives us a status as being newborn Christians. Yet, as infants, we want to be the eyes, ears, hands, and feet as if we know how to hear, see, walk, and talk the moment we are born. Then, we get offended, make assumptions, stumble, and speak without knowledge. This is why it is important to allow God to train and equip us in His ways through our pastors and teachers, mature believers, and time in His word. Ephesians 4:11-12 says, *"And He Himself gave some to be apostles, some prophets, some evangelists, and some pastors and teacher, for the equipping of the saints for the work of ministry, for the edifying of the body of Christ."* We must allow God to place us as the member He has created us to be, so that we will be in His plan, useful for His kingdom, and confident of whom we are in Christ.

Rebekah's Confidence

Much of our confidence comes as we learn and grow. Just as Rebekah witnessed the actions of this servant, she heard his words, and knew the things in her heart, many of us have had this same experience. We have witnessed the actions of someone, heard their words, knowing in our heart that God was speaking to us, but we let something get our focus or we got offended. This is when we build walls against people and God's teachings and we miss out on what God wants for our lives. Rebekah could have gone along with her family and stayed behind, but if she would not have become the wife to Isaac then God would've had to find someone else. Instead, she stayed the course and did not let anything get her focus. She didn't get mad about what was being asked of her. She could have had plans in the works for her life, but God stepped in with a different plan, and the one He had for her was greater than anything she could plan on her own.

God's great plan for us is accomplished each day as we keep Him in our focus, doing what He has asked us to do in that day, each one being different. One day may be cleaning house, another day may be visiting with a friend or family member, and the next day may be in prayer or Bible study all day. Whatever the day brings just keep God in focus. Rebekah didn't lose sight of what was spoken, what she witnessed or how she felt. God was able to fulfill His great plan for her life and she became the mother of a great nation, the nurturer of God's chosen people, and the lineage of our great Lord and Savior, Jesus Christ. What great things could God do with you if you would be more like Rebekah and decide to go with God? No matter where, no matter how, even if you don't understand why. She didn't know that she would be such a great woman for God and that she would fulfill plans and the purposes for His kingdom. She didn't know that her story of confidence would be written in the Bible to encourage us to be more confident. She just followed God.

Don't lose sight of what He has spoken to you about. Don't forget where He has told you to go. Allow yourself to be an infant and learn to become a child. Then allow yourself the time to be that child and learn to become an adult. Don't stay an infant your whole life but desire the pure milk of the word that you may grow as 1 Peter 2:2 says. Growth will come as we are taught, disciplined, instructed, and guided by the truth of God's word through Bible study, prayer, attendance to church, and obedience to all His truths. As we grow into maturity we will start producing fruit in our life. So, don't ignore changes He has asked you to make don't get offended and run, or God will have to find someone else to fulfill the great plan He has for you. You can trust Him with your life.

We have learned here about the sacrifices that came with being in God's plan for Rebekah's life. She would be many miles from her family and have to leave all she had ever known. We saw how much confidence it took for her to know that God was calling her out for a specific ministry, the wife of Isaac. In today's society, women are told that motherhood alone is an unfulfilling job. There's great pressure to go to college and seek a career. Women grow up to think that being "just" a wife and mother without a career is wrong, but God shows us in His word that it is an honorable position.

Rebekah's Confidence

God handpicked Rebekah to be the wife of Isaac because He knew she would do whatever He asked of her. Lord said to Abraham, *"I will establish My covenant with him (Isaac) for an everlasting covenant and with his descendants after him"* Genesis 17:19. This was a chosen family so He needed the perfect woman to fulfill that position; to be the wife of a chosen man and the mother of his descendants. The sacrifice of leaving her family was small in comparison to the blessings she received. Being in God's plan does require something of us and even though that something may seem huge at the time, it becomes small when compared to the blessings that are received. He has a ministry for each of you too, but it is your decision to go. Only you can choose to make the sacrifice to be in His perfect plan.

Decide to go – wherever He leads. Endure the heartache of the sacrifices and great rewards will come in the end. *"For you have need of endurance, so that <u>after</u> you have done the will of God, you may receive the promise: For yet a little while, and He who is coming will come and will not tarry. Now the just shall live by faith; but if anyone draws back, My soul has no pleasure in him"* Hebrews 10:36-38. God is looking for those that will endure to be in His plan, so they can receive the promise. Don't draw back from His plans or you'll miss out on a great life. Let's decide to make changes in our life, to draw closer to the Lord, and be all that He has created us to be. We are the body of Christ, let us not be lame. If each one of us will do all He asks us to do and decide to go wherever He leads, then together, as a body, we can do great things for God and watch Him do great things for us as we grow more confident each day.

Has God spoken to you about something that you have lost sight of? _____

_____

Has He told you to go somewhere, but you have forgotten? _____

_____

What changes has He asked you to make that you have ignored? _____

_____

Will you decide to go with Him no matter where? _____

Do you love God more than yourself? _____

What is your heart's desire? _____

_____

_____

_____

_____

_____

_____

_____

Rebekah's Confidence

God will give you your heart's desire, just be willing to be trained, patient through the trials, and focused on God. Using 1 verse from any 15 different Psalms, create your own 15 verse Psalm asking Him to help you with what He has asked of you and to give you your heart's desire. It does not have to be word for word. You can let the Psalm inspire you to write your own.

Example: 1) In You, O Lord, I put my trust; help me to never shame You. (Psalm 71:1). 2) Lord, You are my refuge and my fortress, My God, in You I will trust. (Psalm 91:2). 3) Bless the Lord, O my soul; and all that is with me, bless Your holy name! (Psalm 103:1).

1. _____
_____
_____
_____

2. _____
_____
_____
_____

3. _____
_____
_____
_____

4. _____
_____
_____
_____

5. _____
_____
_____
_____

6. _____
_____
_____
_____

7. _____
_____
_____
_____

Rebekah's Confidence

8. _____
_____
_____
_____

9. _____
_____
_____
_____

10. _____
_____
_____
_____

11. _____
_____
_____
_____

12. _____
_____
_____
_____

13. _____
_____
_____
_____

14. _____
_____
_____

15. _____
_____
_____
_____

Rebekah's Confidence

Chapter Four

Genesis 24:59-67

> *"So they sent away Rebekah their sister and her nurse, and Abraham's servant and his men. And they blessed Rebekah and said to her: "Our sister, may you become the mother of thousands of ten thousands; and may your descendants possess the gates of those who hate them." Then Rebekah and her maids arose, and they rode on the camels and followed the man. So the servant took Rebekah and departed.*
>
> *Now Isaac came from the way of Beer Lahai Roi, for he dwelt in the South. And Isaac went out to meditate in the field in the evening; and he lifted his eyes and looked, and there, the camels were coming.*
>
> *Then Rebekah lifted her eyes, and when she saw Isaac she dismounted from her camel; for she had said to the servant, "Who is this man walking in the field to meet us?" The servant said, "It is my master." So she took a veil and covered herself. And the servant told Isaac all the things that he had done. Then Isaac brought her into his mother Sarah's tent; and he took Rebekah and she became his wife, and he loved her. So Isaac was comforted after his mother's death.* (NKJV)

4. Respectful Dismount and Covering

It is obvious from this passage that Rebekah's family was not poor. The things given to her family were a dowry which was a provision accorded by law to a wife for her support in the event that she should survive her husband and was agreed upon at the time of the wedding. The nose ring, bracelet, and jewelry given to Rebekah did not make her decision. If we look at her heart we will see more than earthly treasures hidden there. When we first met Rebekah, she was giving water to the thirsty, food to the hungry, and shelter to the needy. God found her faithful in a few things, so He asked a little more, just as He said to the servant with the talents in Matthew 25:23, *"Well done, good and faithful servant; you have been faithful over a few things, I will make you ruler over many things."* Jesus also said in Luke 16:10-12, *"He who is faithful in what is least is faithful also in much; and he who is unjust in what is least is unjust also in much. Therefore if you have not been faithful in the unrighteous mammon, who will commit to your trust the true riches? And if you have not been faithful in what is another man's who will give you what is your own?"*

God saw a woman that was selfless and full of love, one that showed the characteristics of a Christian, who was good and faithful in all that God had asked her to do. She took on the burdens of another man and made them her own. She was confident in her Lord, loved Him and would follow wherever He led. This was a woman He could use for great and wonderful things because she listened and obeyed in all things. This should be a witness to us about who God wants us to be, and the first place He will look is at your heart.

Rebekah's Confidence

Rebekah's heart was beautiful in the sight of the Lord. God found Rebekah faithful in her giving and she did it with a pure heart. She shows outwardly in her body language what her inner heart looked like.

She didn't know Isaac, but she knew this was the man that God had given to her. Her confidence in God gave her the ability to be devoted to him before she even met him. Rebekah knew what devotion looked like. These were not just words from her lips, but an attitude in her heart and a physical action that was seen, because she knew her place as a wife and what God says about that place. *"Wives, submit to your own husbands, as to the Lord"* Ephesians 5:22. *"Wives, submit to your own husbands, as is fitting in the Lord"* Colossians 3:18. We have been told that in submitting to our husbands, we lose our identity and become mindless robots doing what our husbands tell us like little children. We have been told that submitting is being controlled, shows weakness, and puts us in bondage. However, according to God, in submission we gain power, freedom, and strength. This is completely opposite of what we have been taught and it may be hard for us to embrace as truth.

It's like trying to understand how we can gain our life if we lose it for Christ sake (Matthew 10:39). Anyone that has given their life to Christ knows how true this is. When we lose our life and place it in God's hands, and be obedient, we gain a real life that lasts for eternity. The same is true in submission, we gain so much from being submissive and Satan has twisted the meaning to get us to rebel against God's truth. In rebellion, our families are torn apart, because what God intended for couples to do for each other and with each other is destroyed. Then Satan wins in our lives and the lives of our family all because we don't want to be obedient to God's word because of society's definition of submission. We can gain so many of God's promises with this one act of obedience if we will trust what God says in His word; and submit.

For every promise God gives us there is a stipulation of obedience. If you confess and believe, you will be saved. If you will pray and seek My face you will be heard. If you obey My voice and walk in all My ways you will be blessed. When we obey God then He can bless us for our obedience. Obedience is a requirement to walk with God. *"For this is the love of God, that we keep His commandments. And His commandments are not burdensome"* 1 John 5:3. *"And to love Him with all the heart, with all the understanding, with all the soul and with all the strength, and to love one's neighbor as oneself is more than all the whole burnt offerings and sacrifices"* Mark 12:33. To obey God in the fullness of whom we are, we must walk in the place that God commands us to walk. In doing this, we become His secret weapon, a warrior in His kingdom.

There is no greater place to be than a warrior in God's kingdom, but we give that up when we try to make ourselves warriors here on this earth by being rebellious to submission. "I am woman, hear me roar," attitude will get us nowhere with God. He created us with the ingredients of a warrior, this is why we are so strong, able to multi task, and endure many

Rebekah's Confidence

things. There is some truth to the little nursery rhyme that says, "Sugar and spice and everything nice, that's what little girls are made of…snakes and snails and puppy dog tails that's what little boys are made of?" In the beginning, God created us differently, with different ingredients. Man came from the dust of the earth, *"and the Lord God formed man of the dust of the ground, and breathed into his nostrils the breath of life; and man became a living being"* Genesis 2:7. Woman came from man, *"then the rib which the Lord God had taken from man He made into a woman, and He brought her to the man"* Genesis 2:22. We were never meant to be men or hold his position and men were never meant to be women or hold our position. He created us with a different purpose, and we are a secret weapon, if we will walk in our positions.

Sadly, in the fight for equal rights, women have lost their equality. They started taking the position God created for men, which makes them weak and men started giving it, in turn making them weak. Over the generations it has become a way of life. Now our children have no idea what a family created by God looks like. We have gotten our eyes off the ways of God and put them on the ways of man, giving up our priceless position as God's warriors to seek an unfulfilling position that keeps us searching and wanting for more. See, God's definition of equality is all about unity. Equality and unity come when we walk in our own positions.

Rebekah understood what that position meant. It didn't mean being controlled or being robbed of her independence or identity. She was still her own person and Isaac would not change that. She would just become part of his life and he would become part of hers. They would share their lives with each other. Without submission we don't share, we struggle. Our marriage becomes a battleground to gain the highest position where there is **strength** and **power** or so we've been told. We have strength and a power all our own, given to us by God when we walk in the place He created us to walk. We are lead to believe that this great position that God has created for us is a degrading, worthless, and powerless position. So, we fight against it and all the blessings and fulfillments that come with it. Before we can surrender to the submission to our husbands, we have to surrender to the submission of the Lordship of Jesus Christ with our obedience.

Some of us need to respectfully dismount from our position and let our husbands be our covering. Until we do, that unity and equality will never come to our marriage. We will continue to search and struggle, seek and long, but never attain the peace that comes when we find that place God created us to walk in. Rebekah was brought up in a different time. Women were taught the greatness of that place God has for us. Unfortunately, we have not been taught the truth about our position. We have been lied to by the world which has kept women confused about who we really are for God. This lie has kept us searching for something we already had and ultimately gets us to move into a position that makes us weak. In our confusion and weakness God has lost His secret weapon. Rebekah was a secret weapon. She did great things for God, for Isaac, for her family, and for the lineage of our Lord and Savior, Jesus Christ. She did all those amazing things walking in the position

Rebekah's Confidence

God created for her. We can do great things too if we can come to understand our position, submit to it, and become a secret weapon for God.

Will you surrender from the ideas that the world has taught about submission to our husbands and come to the truth of what submission really is? Romans 12:2, *"And do not be conformed to this world, but be transformed by the renewing of your mind, that you may prove what is that good and acceptable and perfect will of God."* It is important that we renew our mind to the ways of Christ according to God's word, not man's ideas. Submission is an area of Scripture that man has tried to conform to the world because women have been offended. However, offense will remove us from God's plan and purpose for our life and submission to our husbands is part of His plan for us. In every area of our life we are submitting to some authority. Our boss at work, a teacher at school, and the policemen on the streets are all people we submit to, but when it comes to submitting to our husband, we think it is degrading, so we rebel. *"For rebellion is as the sin of witchcraft, and stubbornness is as iniquity and idolatry. Because you have rejected the word of the Lord, He also has rejected you from being king"* 1 Samuel 15:23. When we rebel against God's word and become stubborn about what we think, we sin against God and He will reject us just as he did King Saul.

Submission is not an old time teaching that does not apply to us in our new age. Yes, our culture has changed, but our God has not. *"Jesus Christ is the same yesterday, today, and forever"* Hebrews 13:8. What has changed is the definition submission has been given and since we have been lied to about what submission means, we have also been lied to about how to submit. It doesn't mean that we don't get an opinion but that we value our husband's opinion also. It doesn't mean that we can't do what we want but that we consider his feelings in our wants. It doesn't mean that we don't get an opinion, but that we value our husband's opinion also. It doesn't mean that we can't do what we want, but that we consider his feelings in our wants. It doesn't mean that we can't make decisions, but that they are made together. When we submit, it shows respect and honor to the one man we love so much that we committed our life to him. It shows that we have full confidence in his ability to lead the family. It shows that we believe that he will never do anything to hurt us. It shows that we trust that he always has our best interest at heart. When we submit, we allow him to be all that God created him to be.

As we steps into that place as the leader he gains power, freedom, and strength to be a great husband to you. We emasculate our husbands when we do not submit to them and we rob them of the fulfillment of their position as well as our own. Submission will bring unity to your household. There will no longer be a war over who is in charge, who is right or who has the better idea. There will no longer be a competition to see who gets their way. You will become unified, working together for the same purpose and have the best interest of the family as a whole. When our family is in order and unified, then God has His secret weapon when our husbands go to battle. As the spiritual leader of our home, he is on the firing line and we are the secret weapon that can be used to pray, encourage, support, and

Rebekah's Confidence

strengthen. We can be used to bring peace, joy, kindness, love, goodness, and patience to our husbands to keep their spirits lifted. We can be used to bring them confidence that they can do anything and we believe in their ability to be all that God created them to be. We can be amazing women as we submit to our husbands as unto the Lord.

Rebekah was an amazing woman. She was a confident wife and God's secret weapon for Isaac. She dismounted from the camel and covered herself to show her submission which showed respect and honor to Isaac. In turn, Isaac took her and loved her as Christ loved the church and gave Himself for her (Eph. 5:25). They were a couple created by God, focused on God; unified together with God.

1. What does Gen. 2:24, Matt. 19:5, Mk. 10:8 and Eph. 5:31 all have in common? _____
_____

2. What does Eph. 5:23 say? _____
_____

3. What does Eph. 5:24 say? _____
_____

5. Summarize Titus 2:3-5? _____
_____

6. What is the result of the behavior in Titus 2:5? _____

7. So if we do not have this behavior, what happens to God's word? _____

8. What is your desire for your husband? _____
_____

9. How do you want to make him feel? _____
_____

10. When you look at him, who do you see? _____
_____

11. Do you desire to make your husband feel valuable? _____

How can you do that? _____
_____
_____

12. Do you desire to make him feel important? _____

How can you do that? _____
_____
_____

Rebekah's Confidence

13. What does Act 2:17&18 say about God's Spirit? _____

_____

14. In Phil. 4:3, who labored in the gospel? _____

15. Who told all of Samaria about Jesus in John 4:28-29? _____

    What happened in verse 39 because of her? _____

16. Who was it that did something great for Jesus in John 12:3? _____

17. What does Luke 8:1-3 say women did? _____

Each of these women gave something that only they could give. We are all unique, special, and created for a purpose. God has given each of you gifts that are exclusively yours. They don't belong to anyone else. Most of us don't even know that we have gifts because we have been so beat down by the world and people around us. We think that we can't be useful for God because we are women, because we have children, because we have a full time job, and a full time home life. No matter your situation, no matter when, where or how, God believes in you because He has created you for a purpose and has given you gifts to use for Him. The only thing that can hold you back from being all God has created you to be is the big two letter word **IF**. If you will obey His word and take your place, then God can do great things with you and you will become His Secret Weapon, a virtuous warrior.

Here we see Rebekah giving a place to Isaac because she had already given that place to God. She didn't know him, but that didn't matter to her, she knew God. She knew that He had hand selected her for Isaac and that was enough. She displayed all she was in this simple, humble act of dismounting and covering. Her relationship with the Father is what gave her the confidence to do not only this, but everything we have seen her do so far. She believed in God. What does it mean to believe? The Greek definition of believe is to cling to, rely on, and commit oneself unto. If we believe we will cling to God and His word, we will rely on Him for all things and we will commit ourselves to God with our entire life. All this will be seen in how we obey God's word. Not just the parts that feel good, but all of it. Do you believe?

Will you <u>invite</u> Him to stay in your life, every part of it? (Trust in Him) _____

Will you <u>decide</u> to go with God wherever He leads? (Cling to Him) _____

Will you <u>give</u> to others as unto the Lord, in everything? (Rely on Him) _____

Will you <u>respectfully dismount</u> from the controls of your life and give them to God? (Commit unto Him) _____

Rebekah's Confidence

Chapter Five

Genesis 25:19-34

> *This is the genealogy of Isaac, Abraham's son. Abraham begot Isaac. Isaac was forty years old when he took Rebekah as wife, the daughter of Bethuel the Syrian of Padan Aram, the sister of Laban the Syrian. Now Isaac pleaded with the Lord for his wife, because she was barren; and the Lord granted his plea, and Rebekah his wife conceived. But the children struggled together within her; and she said, "If all is well, why am I like this?" So she went to inquire of the Lord. And the Lord said to her: "Two nations are in your womb, two peoples shall be separated from your body; one people shall be stronger than the other, and the older shall serve the younger."*
>
> *So when her days were fulfilled for her to give birth, indeed there were twins in her womb. And the first came out red. He was like a hairy garment all over; so they called his name Esau. Afterward his brother came out, and his hand took hold of Esau's heel; so his name was called Jacob. Isaac was sixty years old when she bore them. So the boys grew. And Esau was a skillful hunter, a man of the field; but Jacob was a mild man, dwelling in tents. And Isaac loved Esau because he ate of his game, but Rebekah loved Jacob.*
>
> *Now Jacob cooked a stew; and Esau came in from the field, and he was weary. And Esau said to Jacob, "Please feed me with that same red stew, for I am weary." Therefore his name was called Edom. But Jacob said, "Sell me your birthright as of this day." And Esau said, "Look, I am about to die; so what is this birthright to me?" Then Jacob said, "Swear to me as of this day." So he swore to him, and sold his birthright to Jacob. And Jacob gave Esau bread and stew of lentils; then he ate and drank, arose, and went his way. Thus Esau despised his birthright. (NKJV)*

5. Went to the Lord

When Isaac took Rebekah for his wife he was 40 years old. We don't know how old Rebekah was, but we do know that 20 years goes by before Jacob and Esau are born because Isaac is 60 years old at their birth. In those twenty years they only had each other. This gave them time to develop their relationship, to grow in their love, and to understand their strengths and weaknesses, but it didn't change the fact that they wanted children. Isaac pleaded with the Lord for Rebekah to conceive. Notice here that it is Isaac who prayed. We don't hear that Rebekah had a complaint, grumble or anything. We have already seen four points of Rebekah's confidence before her union with Isaac. So when it came to this time in her life, she had no doubt that she was right where God wanted her to be. This is where we see more about Rebekah's character. She was content wherever she found herself, from giving water to camels to being barren; she didn't let anything get her ruffled.

Rebekah's Confidence

Paul spoke of this very thing in *Philippians 4:11-13, "Not that I speak in regard to need, for I have learned in whatever state I am, to be content: I know how to be abased, and I know how to abound. Everywhere and in all things I have learned both to be full and to be hungry, both to abound and to suffer need. I can do all things through Christ who strengthens me."* This is the confidence that Rebekah showed. No matter her situation, she was content believing that she could do anything because of the God she served. It also showed her Christ-like attitude as *Hebrews 13:5 says, "Let your conduct be without covetousness, and be content with such things as you have. For He Himself has said, 'I will never leave you nor forsake you'."* Rebekah was confident that her Lord would never leave her nor forsake her. She did what God asked her to do in all things and during those 20 years she had been doing exactly that. God told her be Isaac's wife and she did. That's all God had asked her to do and nothing else. God did not make any other promises to her. The promises that were made by God were made to Isaac, he went to the Lord and the Lord granted his prayer.

However, while pregnant, Rebekah began having some problems. She knew something wasn't right with her pregnancy so she inquired of the Lord, *"If all is well, why am I this way?"* Every woman who has experienced complications of any kind during their pregnancy can understand these feelings. The feelings of uncertainty and fear gets us to start wondering if the baby is okay or if something is wrong with us. Today we can go to the doctor to get our questions answered. We get to see the baby which reassures us of their development. We get to hear the baby's heartbeat which reassures us of their health. We are also informed if we have one, two or six babies in there. These are all conveniences that Rebekah didn't have and we have learned to rely on them instead of God.

We can find an answer to just about any question by typing it into the computer. We can travel to just about anywhere we want to go without much effort by car, plane, train or boat. We can buy just about anything we want with credit. With these conveniences we don't have to pray about what we should do, where we should go, or what we should buy. We do what we want by becoming self-reliant and we place our confidence in ourselves. These conveniences are tools that can be used to help us in life, but they should not take God's place. We should consider God in every situation that arises. *"Trust in the Lord with all your heart, and lean not on your own understanding; in all your ways acknowledge Him, and He shall direct your paths"* Proverbs 3:5-6. Instead, we forget God and rely on our conveniences. We take the tools out of the box and put God in it, and then when all fails, we open the box to let God out, so He can fix things for us. Jesus said in Matthew 19:26 *"that all things are possible with God."* All things are possible, not profitable, 1 Corinthians 10:23, *"All things are lawful for me, but not all things are helpful; all things are lawful for me, but not all things edify."* Philippians 4:13 says, *"I can do all things through Christ who strengthens me,"* but we must let Christ strengthen us, we can't just choose to do things on our own, and then ask God to bless it or fix it. We want to claim all these Scriptures, but we leave God in the box and use the tools our own way. It is important that we understand how to enjoy our conveniences without letting them take God's place in our life and we do this by

Rebekah's Confidence

strengthening our relationship with Him.

Rebekah went to the Lord without our conveniences and we can go to the Lord in the midst of them. It's all about our relationship with Him and the confidence that we gain from that relationship. Rebekah didn't know what was happening to her body or to her child. She didn't know that there was more than one child in her womb; she just knew there was something wrong. Her confidence in the Lord took her to Him in her time of need, and He answered, *"Two nations are in your womb, two peoples shall be separated from your body; one people shall be stronger than the other, and the older shall serve the younger."* She didn't inquire any more information, this gave her peace and there is always peace when God answers. She was satisfied with what God had told her even though she didn't fully understand it. She just accepted that God knew what He was talking about. She believed without seeing and that is faith.

She didn't see anything until they were born. God told her there were two nations in her womb and she could immediately see a difference in their appearance, one being hairy and the other smooth. This was the first confirmation for Rebekah that she really heard God. She believed, waited in faith, and let God prove Himself to her. Then, as the boys grew, she could see more of the words of the Lord being fulfilled. Esau was a skillful hunter and a man of the field, but Jacob was a mild man who dwelled in tents. So, right away in these few Scriptures we see two totally different people, one being physically stronger than the other. Rebekah gained more confidence in the words of the Lord as she watched her boys grow into men.

We have all gone through times in our life when we didn't know if we were hearing from God or answering our own prayers. "God is that You or me?" we ask. If we will do what Rebekah did, pray and wait, then we get the answer to that question. God will do for us what He did for Rebekah and confirm what He has spoken. Our biggest problem is that we get impatient. We want an answer and results right now, but God does not work that way. We have to learn to do things God's way and accept His will and plan. Rebekah has already seen God do great things in her life. She was obedient to do God's will and God was faithful to do more for her than she could ever imagine or hope. *"Now to Him who is able to do exceedingly abundantly above all that we ask or think, according to the power that works in us..."* Ephesians 3:20-21. *"For I know the thoughts that I think toward you, says Lord, thoughts of peace and not of evil, to give you a future and a hope"* Jeremiah 29:11.

God can give us a great future just as He did Rebekah if we are obedient and faithful to Him. *"For there is no partiality with God,"* Romans 2:11. What He does for others He will do for you. Rebekah had a confident relationship with God. She believed, trusted, relied upon, and clung to Him for everything. She had faith. We have seen this in all points of her life and this one is no different. She saw the evidence of what God had spoken to her about the boys when they were born. As they grew older, they began to make decisions and do things on their own to fulfill the words of the Lord without even trying.

Rebekah's Confidence

In verses 29-34, Esau sells his birthright to Jacob. Why did Jacob ask for it? Better question, why did Esau so easily sell it? It never hurts to ask, but why would you give up something so precious. He must not have thought much of it to give it up for a bowl of soup. He had the attitude that he was going to die if he didn't eat at that moment, so he gave up something eternal for something temporal. We look at Esau's action and are appalled, but we aren't any different with our actions. We give up eternal things with God for the temporal things of this world. We give up moving forward with Him and the blessings that He has for us for something miniscule in comparison today. We place our wants and desires before Him. We do this in all different ways: it could be money, careers, friendships, activities, or attitudes. Anything we put before God becomes a temporal thing that we exchange for the eternal.

We get offended at God's word and turn away because it's not what we want to hear and exchange the truth for a lie, Romans 1:21-22. We procrastinate when God says to change and that is exchanging Spirit for flesh, Galatians 5:17-23. We refuse to surrender our life for someone else's then we exchange obedience for disobedience, Matthew 22:37-39. We throw a fit when we don't get our way and exchange our sonship for illegitimacy, Hebrews 12:7-8. We refuse God in many different ways with our attitude and our words. We are giving up eternal things with God for the temporal things of ourselves. Rebekah didn't make any exchanges in her life. She watched and prayed, during which, she grew more confident as the boys began to play out the role God said they would.

She was obedient and faithful to God. God was faithful to her because He had proven Himself as she stepped out in faith and trusted to move forward with Him. In Genesis 24:60, Rebekah's family prayed a blessing on her, *"Our sister, may you become the mother of thousands of ten thousands; and may your descendants possess the gates of those who hate them."* She had lived with Isaac for twenty years without any fulfillment of that blessing, but she did not lose heart. *"Therefore I ask that you do not lose heart at my tribulations for you, which is your glory. For this reason I bow my knees to the Father of our Lord Jesus Christ, from whom the whole family in heaven and earth is named, that He would grant you, according to the riches of His glory, to be strengthened with might through His Spirit in the inner man, that Christ may dwell in your hearts through faith; that you, being rooted and grounded in love, may be able to comprehend with all the saints what is the width and length and depth and height – to know the love of Christ which passes knowledge; that you may be filled with all the fullness of God"* Ephesians 3:13-19. Her faith was seen in her actions, her conduct, and her confidence as she went to the Lord.

1. Explain how Romans 1:21-22 describes exchanging the truth for a lie. _____

_____

_____

_____

_____

Rebekah's Confidence

2. Explain how Galatians 5:17-23 shows the exchange of Spirit for flesh when we do not change._____

_____

_____

_____

3. Explain how Matthew 22:37-39 describes lack of surrender to be exchanging obedience for disobedience. _____

_____

_____

_____

4. Explain how Hebrews 12:7-8 shows refusing correction as exchanging sonship for illegitimacy._____

_____

_____

_____

5. Are you making any of these exchanges in your life? _____

_____

_____

_____

6. Are you letting the temporal things cloud your vision of the eternal? Do you think what God is asking of you is too difficult? _____

_____

_____

_____

7. Are you content with the things that are going on in your life today or do you find yourself getting impatient? _____

_____

_____

_____

8. Do you let the conveniences of this world keep you from going to God for everything? ___

_____

_____

_____

9. Are you confident in your relationship with God to go to Him for anything and believe that He will answer you? _____

10. Do you know how to hear Him when He speaks to you? _____.

Rebekah's Confidence

If you are having trouble in this area of your walk with God then let's take some tips from Rebekah. She contently did what God asked her to do and did it to the best of her ability. She trusted that God would answer her when she went to Him. She waited by being patient, content, and confident in her Lord. Ask God to help you to be content. Ask Him to speak clearly to your heart. Then listen and wait for God to answer as you continue to pray and remember that God will use people to speak to you also.

11. Do you believe God's word for your life? Do you believe that the promises and the blessings He makes are for you as well as others? _____

12. If yes, go to God and ask Him to help you see beyond this time or season of your life to the eternal things He has promised for you. _____

_____

_____

_____

_____

_____

_____

_____

13. Thank Him for some prayers that He has already answered for you? _____

_____

_____

_____

_____

_____

_____

_____

14. Are you patient to wait for God, believing that He is faithful? _____

15. What does 1 Corinthians 1:9 say about God? _____

16. Are you faithful to Him? _____

17. In what ways do you show your faithfulness to Him? _____

_____

_____

_____

18. What does Ephesians 3:20 say about God? _____

_____

_____

_____

Rebekah's Confidence

19. Do you believe that God will do this for you? _____

20. What does Hebrews 11:1 say? _____
_____
_____
_____

21. What does Romans 1:17 say? _____
_____
_____
_____

22. What is the word "it" referring to in this verse? _____

Rebekah's Confidence

Chapter Six

Genesis 26:34-27:13

> *When Esau was forty years old, he took as wives Judith the daughter of Beeri the Hittite, and Basemath the daughter of Elon the Hittite. And they were a grief of mind to Isaac and Rebekah.*
>
> *Now it came to pass, when Isaac was old and his eyes were so dim that he could not see, that he called Esau his older son and said to him, "My son." And he answered him, "Here I am." The he said, "Behold now, I am old, I do not know the day of my death. Now therefore, please take your weapons, your quiver and your bow, and go out to the field and hunt game for me. And make me savory food, such as I love, and bring it to me that I may eat, that my soul may bless you before I die."*
>
> *Now Rebekah was listening when Isaac spoke to Esau his son. And Esau went to the field to hunt game and to bring it. So Rebekah spoke to Jacob her son, saying, "Indeed I heard your father speak to Esau your brother, saying, 'Bring me game and make savory food for me, that I may eat it and bless you in the presence of the Lord before my death.'*
>
> *Now therefore, my son, obey my voice according to what I command you. Go now to the flock and bring me from there two choice kids of the goats, and I will make savory food from them for your father, such as he loves. Then you shall take it to your father, that he may eat it, and that he may bless you before his death."*
>
> *And Jacob said to Rebekah his mother, "Look, Esau my brother is a hairy man, and I am a smooth skinned man. Perhaps my father will feel me, and I shall seem to be a deceiver to him; and I shall bring a curse on myself and not a blessing." But his mother said to him, "Let your curse be on me, my son; only obey my voice, and go, get them for me."* (NKJV)

6. Believed the Lord

When Rebekah went to the Lord in the last chapter, we saw evidence that she believed what the Lord said. She had His words, *"Two nations are in your womb, two peoples shall be separated from your body; one people shall be stronger than the other, and the older shall serve the younger."* She clung to those words. This scene showed Rebekah getting ready to act upon the words of the Lord. As she overheard the conversation between Isaac and Esau, she knew that her husband was getting ready to make a big mistake that would affect the future generations. When she told Jacob what was happening and what she wanted him to do, he was nervous about getting a curse instead of a blessing. He didn't believe that it would work, but Rebekah had no doubt that she was doing the right thing. If fact, she was so sure about it that she was willing to take the curse if anything went wrong. So, no matter the cost to herself, she had a desire to follow through with all that the Lord had

Rebekah's Confidence

laid on her heart from the beginning. This was a consistency in Rebekah's life; she would constantly follow through with all that God asked her to do and believed to be right. Jacob listened to his mother; he heard urgency in her speech, the conviction in her heart, and her willingness to be cursed and he believed in her.

Now, with this scene on hold for just a moment, let's look at the lives of these boys again to give us a better understanding of what Rebekah was about to do. Esau took for himself not one, but two wives. According to Esau, he was the most eligible bachelor in the land. Maybe his head was a little swollen because of his strong stature and his skillful abilities. Ego can get in the way of our better judgment if we are not careful to keep pride out of our lives. Just because we have abilities and skills does not make us better than someone else. We must be careful that we don't take too much credit for the things that God does in our lives and the abilities He gives us. It is very important that we understand that we are fellow workers with God, not lone rangers making a difference for God. 1 Corinthians 3:9, *"for we are God's fellow workers; you are God's field, you are God's building."* Luke 18:27, *"The things which are impossible with men are possible with God."* We have to allow God to be glorified in our life as we work for Him and with Him because without Him we can do nothing. We see with Esau that he did not respect his family or God. He was a lone ranger out to impress his father for material gain and women for physical gain. Not only did he have two wives, but they were both Hittite women. This meant that his blood line would no longer be pure.

Remember why Abraham sent his servant to take a wife from his country and his family, to keep the bloodline pure. Deuteronomy 7:3-4, *"Nor shall you make marriages with them* (Hittite being among a list of 'ites' named in 7:1). *You shall not give your daughter to their son, nor take their daughter for your son. For they will turn your sons away from following Me, to serve other gods; so the anger of the Lord will be aroused against you and destroy you suddenly."* Even though this law had not been set in place yet, God had spoken to Abraham. It could have been destroyed two generations later, if Rebekah had not stepped in to do what was right.

We are not given much information about Jacob except that he was a mild man, dwelling in tents. This tells us that he was quiet and helped his mother around the house. Being quiet is a quality, Proverbs 21:23, *"Whoever guards his mouth and tongue keeps his soul from troubles."* Being helpful is a quality, Galatians 6:2, *"Bear one another's burdens, and so fulfill the law of Christ."* We know that he cooked and we know that he obeyed his mother and father. Ephesians 6:1 states the command, *"Children, obey your parents in the Lord, for this is right."* He was not a hunter, and he was probably not physically strong.

According to 1 Corinthians 1:27, *"But God has chosen the foolish things of the world to put to shame the wise, and God has chosen the weak things of the world to put to shame the things which are mighty."* Just because he did not have the same abilities or skills that Esau had does not mean that he was not strong in some other way. We see through Jacob's actions that he respected his mother and father; therefore, he probably respected God. We also learned in the last chapter that Jacob planned for his future. It takes great patience to work toward something and in our world of "instants" not many of us have patience anymore. We can easily drive to the store to get what we need, so patience is a rarity, but it is a fruit of the Spirit that we should all learn to grow in. So, with all of this information, we can see two completely different personalities in these two brothers.

They have "paved the way" to their future; something the Lord had spoken to Rebekah before their birth. The fruit of their lives was seen by the things they do and the things they say. Rebekah saw their fruit and perhaps Isaac did too, but God had not spoken to Isaac as He did Rebekah, so he did not have the insight that Rebekah had. For Isaac, giving Esau the blessing was the natural thing to do, but if we know anything about God, we know that His ways are not our ways as it says in Isaiah 55:8-9, *"For My thoughts are not your thoughts, nor are your ways My ways, says the Lord. For as the heavens are higher than the earth, so are My ways higher than your ways, and My thoughts than your thoughts."* Esau was the first born and should have been the one to inherit the blessing and all that Isaac had because that was the way things were done.

However, things had already been set in motion by the boys before this time came. Esau sold his birthright and he knew it, but because of his heart he didn't stand by his word and tell his father the truth about selling it. He was full of pride and arrogance. He set out to rob Jacob of what was now rightfully his. Esau exchanged his birthright for something to eat. When he made that exchange, He gave up his rights to the inheritance, just as we can give up our rights to the inheritance with Christ when we exchange it for things of this world. *"Do not lay up for yourselves treasures on earth… but lay up for yourselves treasures in heaven… For where your treasure is, there your heart will be also."* (Matthew 6:19-21) We are making these exchanges in our life every day when we choose lies of man over truths of God.

Exchanging what we want to believe over what God's word says will get us away from God and His promises. We have the Bible which is the very words of God to help us stay on the right path. We can't pick and choose what we want from His word and leave the rest. All of it is His words. 2 Timothy 3:16-17 says, *"All Scripture is given by inspiration of God, and is profitable for doctrine, for reproof, for correction, for instruction in righteousness, that the man of God may be complete, thoroughly equipped for every good work."* We should look to the Scriptures to correct us, instruct us, and prove us so that we may be complete for God. His word gives us all the answers to life and how to live in Christ before God our Father. Hebrews 4:12 says, *"For the word of God is living and powerful, and sharper than any two-edged sword, piercing even to the division of soul and spirit, and of joints and marrow, and is a discerner of the thoughts and intents of the heart."* God's living word is truth and should not be exchanged for anything. It is important to obey God in all areas of our lives.

God's word tells us that Rebekah loved Jacob more, that the Hittite women were a grief to her; however, she knew that the Lord had spoken to her while she was still pregnant. She never forgot His words, she believed them, and based on all we know about her, we can determine that her desire was to obey Him. Many sermons have been preached about the deception of Rebekah, and still more about Jacob being a deceiver, but let's ask this question. What would have happened if Esau had gotten the blessing? We will never know because Rebekah took action. Yes, she used deception, but she should not be defined solely on this one act. Maybe she should have fell on her knees in prayer, cried out to God for a miracle, but she panicked and took control of the situation. How many of us are guilty of the same things, but none of us want to be defined by our mistakes. Sadly, this is the main characteristic that we hear about Rebekah and we miss learning from her great faith, sacrificial obedience, and strong confidence in the Lord.

Isaac was not seeing things clearly and he was only doing what was custom for the first born. He was not looking to what this blessing was going to do to their family and future generations. God needed a man of character and Jacob's heart showed the character of a man that planned for the future and respected his parents. He held his tongue, followed instruction, and bore some of the family burdens. God needed a humble man with integrity, purity, and good fruit in his heart. *Romans 2:13-16, For not the hearers of the law are just in the sight of God, but the doers of the law will be justified; for when Gentiles, who do not have the law, by nature do the things contained in the law, these, although not having the law are a law to themselves, who show the work of the law written in their hearts, their conscience also bearing witness, and between themselves their thoughts accusing or else excusing them in the day when God will judge the secrets of men by Jesus Christ, according to my gospel."*

We could pretend to be born again just as Esau pretended to have his birthright. We could look good on the outside just as Esau looked like a good strong man. We could seem to others to have what it takes to do the job just as Esau seemed to Isaac. However, God knew the truth about him; in his inward parts and He knows the truth about you because he sees the secrets of our heart whether good or bad. Nothing is hidden from God as Luke 8:17 says, *"For nothing is secret that will not be revealed, nor anything hidden that will not be known and come to light."* Also, Hebrews 4:13 says, *"And there is no creature hidden from His sight, but all things are naked and open to the eyes of Him to whom we must give account."* Jacob may be known as the deceiver but Esau was the one who lived the life of deception; pretending on the outside, but God saw his heart.

This should be a warning to us all, that we can be hiding things in our heart and pretend that God can't see them. His word tells us that He can see the secrets, intents, and motivations of our heart and that is the only place He looks. In 1 Samuel 16:7 the Lord says to Samuel, *"Do not look at his appearance or at his physical stature, because I have refused him. For the Lord does not see as man sees; for man looks at the outward appearance, but the Lord looks at the heart."*

Rebekah's Confidence

Each day we live before God with our hearts naked and our secrets revealed. Ecclesiastes 12:13-14, *"Let us hear the conclusion of the whole matter: Fear God and keep His commandments, for this is man's all. For God will bring every work into judgment, including every secret thing, whether good or evil."* One day we will stand face to face with Him with our hearts naked and our secrets exposed and although that's how he sees us every day, we still have an opportunity to let Him cleanse our hearts and heal us from all unrighteousness. But, that day, when face to face, it will be too late to repent. Now is the time to examine your heart and see what God sees, to ask Him to forgive you and to change your heart. The only way our heart will change is to ask Jesus Christ to be our Lord and Savior, surrender to His will for our lives and follow Him.

It is very simple to ask Jesus Christ to be Lord of your life.

1. Do you truly believe that Jesus is the Son of God? _____

2. Do you truly believe that Jesus died on a cross to redeem us from our sins? _____

3. Do you truly believe that Jesus rose from the dead? _____

If you do agree with these truths of God's word, call upon the Lord Jesus now to forgive you and to save you. Romans 10:13, *"For whoever calls on the name of the Lord shall be saved."* When you call upon Him:

1. You must repent (turn from) your sins.

Acts 3:19, *"Repent therefore and be converted, that your sins may be blotted out, so that times of refreshing may come from the presence of the Lord."*

2. Ask God to forgive you for these sins.

James 1:21 *"Therefore lay aside all filthiness and overflow of wickedness and receive with meekness the implanted word, which is able to save your souls."*

3. Receive Him into your heart.

Act 2:38, *"Then Peter said to them, 'Repent, and let every one of you be baptized in the name of Jesus Christ for the remission of sins; and you shall receive the gift of the Holy Spirit."*

John 3:3, *"Jesus answered, 'Most assuredly, I say to you, unless one is born again (Greek: born from above), he cannot see the kingdom of God.'"*

Rebekah's Confidence

If you have taken this step there are a few things that you should know:

1. God loves you.

John 3:16, *"For God so loved the world that He gave His only begotten Son, that whoever believes in Him should not perish but have everlasting life. For God did not send His Son into the world to condemn the world, but that the world through Him might be saved."*

2. He wants a relationship with you.

Romans 5:10-11, *"For if when we were enemies we were reconciled to God through the death of His Son, much more, having been reconciled, we shall be saved by His life. And not only that, but we also rejoice in God through our Lord Jesus Christ, through whom we have now received the reconciliation."*

3. He has a purpose and a plan for your life.

Jeremiah 29:11, *"For I know the thoughts that I think toward you, says the Lord, thoughts of peace and not of evil, to give you a future and a hope."*

Now that you know some things about God, here are some expectations He has laid out in His word for us to follow as Christians.

1. Develop your relationship with God.

This is done through prayer and Bible study. Prayer is your only way of communicating to God. He can, however, speak to us in many ways: audibly, a still small voice in your heart, through a sermon, through His written word, and many other ways that you will recognize as you grow. The best way to hear from God is through His word so it is important that you read your Bible. Open it every day, not just on Sundays. A good way to start reading is to take notes on Sunday, find the Scriptures that were taught and read the verses before and after. Then look up references which go with the Scriptures to help you understand more. 2 Timothy 3:16, *"All Scripture is given by inspiration of God, and is profitable for doctrine, for reproof, for correction, for instruction in righteousness, that the man of God may be complete, thoroughly equipped for every good work."*

2. Be found faithful to God.

As you learn and grow in your relationship you will find that God expects obedience. We just read in 2 Timothy, the Scriptures are for correction and instruction in righteousness, so that you may be complete and equipped for good works. Obey the Scriptures and use them as a guide for how to live this new life with God. Let God find you faithful every day of your new life with Him so that when you stand before Him on that Day He will say, "well done My good and faithful servant, enter into the joy of your Lord." Matthew 25:21.

3. **Become a disciple.**

This is one of the most important steps you can take in your Christian walk. A disciple means a learner. Become a learner of what God says in His word. You will need to learn how to live a Christian life. It does not automatically come after your prayer. Find a church where the word of God is taught and fellowship with other believers. Hebrews 10:24-25, *"And let us consider one another in order to stir up love and good works, not forsaking the assembling of ourselves together, as is the manner of some, but exhorting one another, and so much the more as you see the Day approaching."*

God is looking for a humble vessel that will learn His ways. He wants someone that will build a relationship with Him and obey everything He says to do. John 14:21, *"He who has My commandments and keeps them, it is he who loves Me. And he who loves Me will be loved by My Father, and I will love him and manifest Myself to him."* Saying a prayer is only the beginning to a new life. This new life is not easy because it is completely different than the way you have been living. We have habits and attitudes from our old life that we will have to learn to deal with. That is why the steps are so important. Just like everything else in life, there are rules. To be a disciple we have to close our mouth and open our ears to hear, not just with our mind, but with our hearts. James 1:19, *"So then, my beloved brethren, let every man be swift to hear, slow to speak, slow to wrath."* To have a relationship, we have to discipline our time to spend it with Him and to be found faithful we have to obey all that God says to do, from attending church and tithing to forgiving others and loving our neighbor. We can look at Rebekah and see that she had a relationship with God because what we see in her life comes from her heart. When she stands before Him on the Day of Judgment she will probably hear, "Well done My good and faithful servant." What will you hear on that Day?

On that Day, what will you hear? How do you work, act, and give to God?

Begrudgingly? "I'll give, but just what is required?" This describes a person that finds excuses why they can't give their entire tithe, time, energy, and all of their heart.

Controlled? "I'll give, but I want to have a say in where every cent goes?" This describes a person that wants to be in control of where their money goes, how they spend their time, and what they do for God. It has to be their way, not Gods.

Boastfully? "I'll give, but not without letting people know what I gave?" This describes a person that cannot quietly or anonymously give anything. They let others know how much they give of their money, time, and energy all the while making a big deal about what they do in their church or ministry.

Freely? "I'll give to God everything that I have, starting with my wallet?" This describes a person that just wants to please God, no matter what He asks of them. They give Him everything; including all of their heart.

Rebekah's Confidence

How are you giving to God? Remember, He knows the truth. _____

_____

_____

_____

What promises do we have in giving according to Luke 6:38? _____

_____

_____

_____

Write what Philippians 4:19 says. _____

_____

_____

_____

Read 2 Corinthians 9:6-8. What does God say to you through these verses? _____

_____

_____

_____

"There is no better indicator of growth in the new life than in the area of giving. *These passages* deals with the attitude one should have in his giving; it should be cheerful. When giving is cheerful, it will also be generous. The important rule of thumb is not how much is given, but how much is left after the giving. God is not primarily occupied with the amount of the gift, but with the motive that lies behind it. All the money in the world belongs to God. My gift to Him does not make Him any richer; it makes me richer spiritually because of the realization that everything I have is His and that I am giving because I love Him and want to give." "Failure to give of the money which God has given is a serious matter. The person who fails to honor God with his money actually robs God, not because it impoverishes God but because it denies the God-ordained means for the support of His work and His ministers. For the child of God who honors God with his money God promises abundant blessings and the provision of his every need." (Open Bible page 1372)

Read Malachi 3:8-10. Write down what we must do to receive the promises. _____

_____

_____

_____

Write down the promises for our obedience. _____

_____

_____

_____

What do you think God is really after from us? _____

Rebekah's Confidence

Rebekah's heart was pure before the Lord. She loved Him and obeyed all He set before her to do. She gave God all her heart.

What does your heart look like before the Lord? _____

Will you <u>really</u> do all that He asks, no matter the cost to yourself? _____

What did the Lord say in 1 Samuel 16:7? _____
_____
_____
_____

Esau tried to impress those around him. Who do you try to impress? _____
_____
_____

What gain do you hope to achieve? _____

Do you "plan for the future" or "live in the moment?" _____

If you plan for the future, what future plans do you have with God? _____
_____
_____
_____

Have you ever been a "lone ranger" for the Lord? _____

What does 1 Cor. 3:9 say? _____
_____
_____
_____

In what ways has pride caused destruction in your life? _____
_____

What does Proverbs 16:18 say? _____
_____

In what ways did God humble you? _____
_____

What does Hebrews 12:11 say? _____
_____
_____

Rebekah's Confidence

How can you use these humbling experiences to glorify God? _____

_____

_____

Do you believe the Lord when He speaks? _____. How does He speak to you? _____

_____

_____

_____

How do you respond to Him? _____

_____

_____

Rebekah's Confidence

Chapter Seven

Genesis 27:14-40

And he (Jacob) went and got them (kid goats) and brought them to his mother, and his mother made savory food, such as his father loved. Then Rebekah took the choice clothes of her elder son Esau, which were with her in the house, and put them on Jacob her younger son. And she put the skins of the kids of the goats on his hands and on the smooth part of his neck. Then she gave the savory food and the bread, which she had prepared, into the hand of her son Jacob.

So he went to his father and said, "My father." And he said, "Here I am. Who are you, my son?" Jacob said to his father, "I am Esau your firstborn; I have done just as you told me; please arise, sit and eat of my game, that your soul may bless me." But Isaac said to his son, "How is it that you have found it so quickly, my son?" And he said, "Because the Lord your God brought it to me." Then Isaac said to Jacob, "Please come near, that I may feel you, my son, whether you are really my son Esau or not." So Jacob went near to Isaac his father, and he felt him and said, "The voice is Jacob's voice, but the hands are the hands of Esau." And he did not recognize him, because his hands were hairy like his brother Esau's hands; so he blessed him. Then he said, "Are you really my son Esau?" He said, "I am." He said, "Bring it near to me, and I will eat of my son's game, so that my soul may bless you." So he brought it near to him, and he ate; and he brought him wine, and he drank.

Then his father Isaac said to him, "Come near now and kiss me, my son." And he came near and kissed him; and he smelled the smell of his clothing, and blessed him and said: "Surely, the smell of my son is like the smell of a field which the Lord has blessed. Therefore may God give you of the dew of heaven, of the fatness of the earth, and plenty of grain and wine. Let peoples serve you, and nations bow down to you. Be master over you brethren, and let your mother's sons bow down to you. Cursed be everyone who curses you, and blessed be those who bless you!"

Now it happened, as soon as Isaac had finished blessing Jacob, and Jacob had scarcely gone out from the presence of Isaac his father, that Esau his brother came in from his hunting. He also had made savory food, and brought it to his father, and said to his father, "Let my father arise and eat of his son's game, that your soul may bless me." And his father Isaac said to him, "Who are you?" So he said, "I am your son, your firstborn, Esau." Then Isaac trembled exceedingly, and said, "Who? Where is the one who hunted game and brought it to me? I ate all of it before you came, and I have blessed him – and indeed he shall be blessed." When Esau heard the words of his father, he cried with an exceedingly great and bitter cry, and said to his father, "Bless me – me also, O my father!" But he said, "Your brother came with deceit and has taken away your blessing." And Esau said, "Is he not rightly named Jacob? For he has supplanted me these two times. He took away my birthright, and now look, he has taken away my blessing!" And he said, "Have you not reserved a blessing for me?"

Then Isaac answered and said to Esau, "Indeed I have made him your master, and all his brethren I have given to him as servants; with grain and wine I have sustained him. What shall I do now for you, my son?" And Esau said to his father, "Have you only one blessing, my father? Bless me – me also, O my father!" And Esau lifted up his voice and wept. Then Isaac his father answered and said to him: "Behold, your dwelling shall be of the fatness of the earth, and of the dew of heaven from above. By your sword you shall live and you shall serve your brother; and it shall come to pass when you become restless, that you shall break his yoke from your neck." (NKJV)

7. Fulfilled His Words

Rebekah believed the Lord when she prayed, Genesis 25:22-23, she went to inquire of the Lord and He answered her. In her belief she took action that fulfilled the words of the Lord. This is true for us also; we will fulfill the words of the Lord for our life if we believe those words and obey them. If God told you to be a missionary in Africa, would you become a Sunday school teacher at your local church? If you believed that God was speaking to you, it is more likely that you would find out what was legally required to travel to Africa. You would seek out other missionaries to gain knowledge from their experiences. You would not just sit back and let life happen to you. You would take charge of the situation and prepare to go to Africa with all that God said to do. God will not pick you up and transport you. It would be up to you to put actions to what God told you to do.

There are no indications that the Lord told Rebekah to take action through deception, it would not be in God's character to do so. But, if we look at Rebekah based on what we have already learned about her, then we have to know that her heart was to obey God. She believed Him and walked by faith, even if she didn't do everything right. If we examined our own lives, from the time of salvation to the moment these words are revealed on this page, we may be able to relate to Rebekah. Maybe we can remember a time that; in zeal for God, with the best intentions, desiring to do what's right, we completely failed, did the opposite of what we should have and hurt others in the process. Knowing that Rebekah's heart was to obey God will keep us from thinking more highly of ourselves than we ought. We are all fallible, but God is sufficient to take our blunders and make them blessings. His desire is for us to know Him and the commandments He gives needs action that should draw us closer to Him.

Jesus said in Matthew 7:26-27, *"Now everyone who hears these sayings of Mine, and does not do them, will be like a foolish man who built his house on the sand: and the rain descended, the floods came, and the winds blew and beat on that house; and it fell. And*

Rebekah's Confidence

great was its fall." Jesus says we are foolish and will fall greatly if we do not do what He says. James 1:22 says if we are hearers and not doers we deceive ourselves. In deceiving ourselves, we refuse God's word which is used to correct and instruct our lives. When we tell our children to do something, we expect them to do it. God tells us to do many things in His word and He expects us to do them.

If our children don't obey us, we punish them for their disobedience, so if we don't obey God through His word, shouldn't we expect punishment? Do we get mad and rebel, throw a little fit, call the rest of the congregation to see if we can get anyone to be on our side? Don't we want someone to tell us it is not our fault so we can feel better? Our kids do the same thing, "Daddy, Mommy spanked me and made me go to bed," hoping that Daddy will say, "That's not right Mommy, you don't do that." Correction is part of being a child, Hebrews 12:7-8 says, *"If you endure chastening, God deals with you as with sons; for what son is there whom a father does not chasten? But if you are without chastening, of which all have become partakers, then you are illegitimate and not sons."* It is important that we endure the chastening and take our correction. As we chasten our children, they become more and more obedient and that is what God is looking for in us.

Obedience is the key to fulfilling God's promises in our lives. He promises us many great things, but we only receive them if we obey. The biggest word in the Bible is "IF". This brings the responsibility back on us to follow through. Rebekah was taking responsibility for what the Lord had spoken. She did not just sit back and let life happen to her and her family. Jesus showed us the difference between good and faithful servants and lazy and wicked servants when he told the parable of the talents in Matthew 25:14-30. He gave talents to three men; two of the men went to work with the talents he gave them. The one that didn't do anything with it, he was called a wicked and lazy servant and was cast into the outer darkness. Sitting back and waiting for God to do everything for us is lazy. Laziness will get you cast into the outer darkness, away from the presence of God and His blessings. It is important to put actions to our lives as we listen to God speak to us. If we know what God says but don't do anything about it, we hinder God's plan for our lives and the lives of others.

Rebekah took matters into her own hands to fulfil the words of the Lord. She intended to protect her family and the future that God had planned for them. God was counting on her to secure the future of His chosen people. The scriptures don't tell us what the Lord asked her to do in the moment she heard of the blessing. We don't know the thoughts that went through her mind. We only remember Rebekah for this act of deception and call her a deceitful woman. We teach others about her deception, but leave out how important it was that Jacob be the one to receive the blessing. How sad that her mistake has become her reputation.

Esau's blood line was no longer pure and he sold his birthright which showed that he didn't value it. She wanted to please God more than her own husband. We hear that the only reason Jacob got the blessing was because he was Rebekah's favorite. No, he was God's

Rebekah's Confidence

chosen. We don't hear about all the wonderful things she did for God and her family. We forget her kindness as she gave water to a man's camels. We forget the sacrifice she made to invite strangers to stay in her home. We forget the faith she had to follow God hundreds of miles away from all she had known. We forget her humility as she showed respect to a stranger husband. Yes, she used deception in this situation and because of that we think something horrible happened to that wonderful camel waterer. It's sad how we focus on mistakes and failures of others, and probably ourselves too, instead of the good.

We also must remember that God is sufficient in all things. Just because we think what someone does is wrong doesn't mean they are wrong. God's ways don't look like man's ways. What looks wrong in the eyes of man may be right in the eyes of God. Regardless of what we think, Rebekah got the job done, maybe the wrong way, it probably cost her more than we know. But her belief in the Lord can be seen by her consistent lifestyle of obedience and humility. The Lord had spoken to her about the two boys, *"Two nations are in your womb, two peoples shall be separated from your body; one people shall be stronger than the other, and the older shall serve the younger."* The actions of these two boys lined up over the years, with what the Lord spoke. Rebekah believed that Jacob had to receive that blessing; he was the younger and Esau will serve him just as the Lord had said. Could she reason with Isaac about this, would he listen, or were his ears closed because of tradition?

Jesus said in Mark 7:9, *"All too well you reject the commandment of God that you may keep your tradition."* It was the tradition that the first born receive the blessing. In Isaac's blindness, he walked in the traditions of men, but in Rebekah's faith, she fulfilled the words of the Lord, *"the older shall serve the younger"*, even at the cost of her relationship with her husband and her children. This was bigger than her comfort; it was the future of a nation. God can fulfill His plans with or without you. However, if He has to do it without you, then you miss out on the blessings and His plans for your personal life cannot be fulfilled. You can never stop Him from fulfilling His overall plan. He will just find someone else to do the job and give them the blessing that goes with it.

When Isaac blessed Jacob, he said, *"Let your mother's sons bow down to you."* When he spoke to Esau, he said, *"You shall serve your brother."* Because of the action Rebekah took, the correct blessing got to the correct son. We know that Jacob and Esau were over 40 years old, but Rebekah never forgot what the Lord had told her while she was pregnant. It's sad to say, but many of us forget what God has spoken to us before the week is out. We all know people who have had experiences with God, but it never changes their life. They forget what He said, so they never fulfill the words of the Lord in their life. How can we be fellow workers with God if we are not remembering what He tells us? Maybe we go to church every Sunday Morning and hear a message from God, but by Monday we have forgotten what that message was and how we could apply it to our lives. Maybe we attend a Bible Study where lots of information is shared, but rather than look at how it can change our life, we focus on the historical facts that are found.

Rebekah's Confidence

The Bible is not a history book; it is the living word of God. We think if He doesn't come down out of heaven, stand before us, and proclaim what we should do then we are not hearing from Him. The truth is that we hear God every time we read or hear His word. So, if we think we can't hear God, it's more likely that we are simply not receiving what He says. Maybe we hear God speak, but because it costs us something to fulfill His words we pretend we don't hear Him. Maybe we refuse to accept His words because it means that we will have to change. If we wanted to hear Him we would be seeking Him while He may be found. Rebekah sought the Lord when she was pregnant and He spoke. She listened, remembered, and fulfilled all that He said.

Rebekah didn't set out to deceive her husband when God spoke to her 40 years ago, but when she was faced with the situation that required attention; she acted. God may have had a different plan if she had prayed. This is why it is important for us to stay prayed up at all times. Spend time every day in prayer to speak to God, and through Bible study, hear from God. We may have to act on a moment's notice and we must know God's will to react in obedience. Sometimes we don't understand the sacrifice of obedience when God speaks to us until we have obeyed, then we are faced with the cost. Our obedience may look crazy, stupid or even deceptive to the world, but only God knows the intent of our heart.

God can do whatever He wants but for Him to work great things in your life you have to be obedient at all cost. When God is working in our lives there is usually an expectation on us to do something. What are some expectations God has put on us as His children? Obedience is the first and most important, but what all does this involve?

1. _____ (Malachi 3:10)

2. _____ (Matthew 3:11)

3. _____ (Matthew 26:26-28)

4. _____ (Matthew 22:37)

5. _____ Matthew 22:39)

See how many more you can find in Matthew chapters 5-7.

_____
_____
_____
_____
_____
_____
_____
_____

Rebekah's Confidence

Where are you disobedient? What can you do to change your disobedience to God?

_____

_____

_____

_____

_____

_____

_____

_____

_____

Chapter Eight

Genesis 27:41-28:9

So Esau hated Jacob because of the blessing with which his father blessed him, and Esau said in his heart, "The days of mourning for my father are at hand; then I will kill my brother Jacob." And the words of Esau her older son were told to Rebekah. So she sent and called Jacob her younger son, and said to him, "Surely your brother Esau comforts himself concerning you by intending to kill you. Now therefore, my son, obey my voice; arise, flee to my brother Laban in Haran. And stay with him a few days, until your brother's fury turns away, until your brother's anger turns away from you and he forgets what you have done to him; then I will send and bring you from there. Why should I be bereaved also of you both in one day?"

And Rebekah said to Isaac, "I am weary of my life because of the daughters of Heth; if Jacob takes a wife of the daughters of the land, what good will my life be to me?" The Isaac called Jacob and blessed him, and charged him, and said to him; "You shall not take a wife from the daughters of Canaan. Arise, go to Padan Aram, to the house of Bethuel your mother's father; and take yourself a wife from there of the daughters of Laban your mother's brother. May God Almighty bless you, and make you fruitful and multiply you, that you may be an assembly of peoples; and give you the blessing of Abraham, to you and your descendants with you, that you may inherit the land in which you are a stranger, which God gave to Abraham."

So Isaac sent Jacob away, and he went to Padan Aram, to Laban the son of Bethuel the Syrian, the brother of Rebekah, the mother of Jacob and Esau. Esau saw that Isaac had blessed Jacob and sent him away to Padan Aram to take himself a wife from there, and that as he blessed him he gave him a charge, saying, "You shall not take a wife from the daughters of Canaan," and that Jacob had obeyed his father and his mother and had gone to Padan Aram. Also Esau saw that the daughters of Canaan did not please his father Isaac. So Esau went to Ishmael and took Mahalath the daughter of Ishmael, Abraham's son, the sister of Nebajoth, to be his wife in addition to the wives he had. (NKJV)

8. Endured to the End

Rebekah was told the words of Esau and that he intended to kill Jacob. With this knowledge, she reacted with wisdom. She did not let the information get her emotions stirred up. She didn't let her feelings get in the way of facts. Women are known to let emotions move us to do things we wouldn't normally do. In emotions we gain strength that we can say and do anything because this is how we feel and we are going to express those feelings. It is a false sense of strength that usually gets us into trouble later. This is why we are criticized during our ovulation of being hormonal. We are more sensitive to our emotions during this

Rebekah's Confidence

time and let them move us. We are more likely to make decisions based on emotion than on facts. It's just how we are designed.

Emotions are not bad for us to have, God gave them to us. When we love, we love with emotion. When we cry, we cry with emotion. When we care, we care with emotion. When we live, we live with emotion. There is nothing wrong with us having emotions; they are part of being human. However, we should not let emotions run our life. If we make decisions based on our emotions we will not be consistent in our living, because our emotions will keep us tossed. One day we may feel this way and the next day we may feel that way. Our life will feel like a rollercoaster ride, up one day, down the next. To get past emotional decision making takes prayer. Ask God to show you how to make the decision before you do anything, before you say anything. Wait and get the facts before you react to anything with your actions or your words. God will help you if you just ask. James 1:5 says, *"If any of you lacks wisdom, let him ask of God, who gives to all liberally and without reproach, and it will be given to him."* He will help you to react in wisdom just as Rebekah did.

1. When faced with situations in your life, do you react in your emotion (feelings) or do you react in wisdom? _____

_____

_____

_____

2. How can you learn to make better decisions based on wisdom? _____

_____

_____

_____

3. What things can you do to discipline yourself from your emotions? _____

_____

_____

_____

4. We learned all the different kinds of wisdom defined in the Bible. Review the Scriptures and your life, based on what God's word says, which wisdom do you have? _____

_____

_____

_____

5. Are you willing to seek true wisdom that comes from above? _____

6. What does that wisdom look like? _____

_____

_____

_____

Rebekah's Confidence

7. Are you pure, peaceable, gentle, willing to yield, and full of mercy? _____

8. Do you have good fruits without partiality or hypocrisy? _____

9. What changes can you make to have God's wisdom? _____

_____

_____

_____

_____

_____

It takes some discipline to learn to keep our emotions under control and women who have practiced that discipline make better decisions in their life. How many times are we given information and react in our flesh? Emotions can get the best of us if we are not careful. We get angry and lash out or we get hurt and run to hide. We have probably been known to get self-righteous and rehearse our speech of defense. Our reactions show what is really in our hearts, but Rebekah reacted in wisdom. She approached Isaac with a concern about the Canaanite women that they lived among. Jacob must not marry any of these women because his blood line must stay pure. The intent behind her urgency was to get Isaac to send Jacob away so that he was out of Esau's reach. This was a very wise approach for Rebekah because she not only saved Jacob's life, but secured his future.

Wisdom is the result of applying knowledge. The purpose of going to college is to gain knowledge in a specific field. As we gain knowledge, we apply that knowledge and become wise in that field. So, when we apply knowledge to our Christian walk, we obtain wisdom. Knowledge comes when we learn about God's word and how He expects us to live as Christians. We obtain wisdom when we apply that knowledge to our lives. Rebekah obtained wisdom the same way we do; she applied knowledge. If we could master this art of applying knowledge, we could be very wise Christian women.

The Bible tells us that there are different kinds of wisdom. We can have worldly wisdom, our own wisdom, wisdom of this age, and wisdom of men. Proverbs 3:7 says, *"Do not be wise in your own eyes; fear the Lord and depart from evil."* Part of being wise is the fear of the Lord. Romans 12:16 says *"Do not be wise in your own opinion."* So, it is possible for us to think ourselves wise, but really not have any wisdom at all. 1 Corinthians 3:18-20 says, *"Let no one deceive himself. If anyone among you seems to be wise in this age, let him become a fool that he may become wise. For the wisdom of this world is foolishness with God. For it is written, 'He catches the wise in their own craftiness.' And again, 'The Lord knows the thoughts of the wise, that they are futile.'"*

These Scriptures show that our opinion; what we think we know, can deceive us, and that worldly wisdom has nothing to do with God's wisdom. 1 Corinthians 2:5 says, *"That your faith should not be in the wisdom of men but in the power of God."* We cannot comprehend God with our minds based on head knowledge. 1 Corinthians 1:20-21 & 25 says, *"Where is the wise? Where is the scribe? Where is the debater of this age? Has not God made foolish the wisdom of this world? For since, in the wisdom of God, the world through wisdom did not know God, it pleased God through the foolishness of the message preached to save those who believe. Because the foolishness of God is wiser than men and the weakness of God is stronger than men."* Wisdom of the world will not understand God and think the message preached is foolishness. James 3:13-16, *"Who is wise and understanding among you? Let him show by good conduct that his works are done in the meekness of wisdom. But if you have bitter envy and self-seeking in your hearts, do not boast and lie against the truth. This wisdom does not descend from above, but is earthly, sensual, demonic. For where envy and self-seeking exist, confusion and every evil thing are there."*

So, how can we receive the wisdom of God? We have to know what the wisdom of God looks like. James 3:17, *"But the wisdom that is from above is first pure, then peaceable, gentle, willing to yield, full of mercy and good fruits, without partiality and without hypocrisy."* If it doesn't look like this then it is probably not the wisdom of God. This all looks foolish to the world. 1 Corinthians 1:30-31 says, *"But of Him you are in Christ Jesus, who became for us wisdom from God and righteousness and sanctification and redemption that, as it is written, 'He who glories, let him glory in the Lord.'"* The only way to receive God's wisdom is to receive God's Son, Jesus Christ, who gave to us not only wisdom but righteousness, sanctification, and redemption. How do we apply these teaching to our lives? First, we have to hear them, James 1:19-20, *"So then, my beloved brethren, let every man be swift to hear, slow to speak, slow to wrath; for the wrath of man does not produce the righteousness of God."* Then, we have to receive them, James 1:21, *"Therefore lay aside all filthiness and overflow of wickedness, and receive with meekness the implanted word, which is able to save your souls."* Then, we have to live by them, James 1:22, *"But be doers of the word, and not hearers only, deceiving yourselves."* We can then become wise Christian women, not perfect, but equipped to know wisdom in the fear of the Lord.

Many times when we lean on our own understanding and make a mistake, we give up, but not Rebekah. She sees what a mess this has turned into and now that Jacob has the blessing, her whole family is torn apart. She could self-focus and determine that she causes more problems than she solves, but instead she finds a way to continue working toward the goal of securing God's pure bloodline. Sometimes when God gives us a job to do, it seems to never end and we grow tired. Galatians 6:9 says, *"And let us not grow weary while doing good, for in due season we shall reap if we do not lose heart."*

When we give our life to Christ to become a Christian, we give our entire life, not just Sundays. To be a Christian means that you act like the people that followed Christ, in their attitude, not their works. Everyone has not been promised the same abilities as Peter, James, John, or Paul, but we can have their same attitude. Just like Jesus, their attitude was surrender to the will of God and God is looking for a surrendered attitude in us. Rebekah had an attitude of surrender; a lifelong commitment to endure to the end no matter the cost. She gave up her own wants and desires to do what God needed her to do. She probably never

Rebekah's Confidence

saw Jacob again and her heart ached to say goodbye, however, she knew he had to fulfill his purpose now for God. She did her job in securing his future just as Abraham secured Isaac's future when he sent the servant for her. When we do for God it usually benefits the life of someone else so obeying Him at all costs and enduring to the end requires having an attitude of surrender.

Surrendering to God in our lives will give us a blessed life that will overflow into the lives of others. With surrendered hearts, we can live our life for Christ without giving up, losing heart, growing weary or walking away. It is important for us to endure to the end of everything God puts before us, even our trials, Romans 5:3 says, *"we also glory in tribulations, knowing that tribulation produces perseverance; and perseverance, character; and character, hope."* Only if we persevere will we gain character and find hope. Everything has a purpose; so look to see how we can learn (knowledge), and grow (wisdom), and find a closer relationship with God through it. Satan gets too much credit in our lives when we go through trials. We ignore the fact that God may be testing us. Even if Satan is attacking, like he did Job, we can learn something from it, grow closer to God through it, and come out better in the end. The only way this is possible is to have a surrendered attitude and with that we will endure to the end of a trial, the end of our life or the end of time when Jesus returns.

Rebekah did not see the end of time but she did endure to the end of her trials and the end of her life. Everything she did was for God and she lost her reputation because of it. She lost her last days with Jacob and possibly had an angry husband to contend with. No matter how hard this was for her, she was confident in her Lord, and in who she was. She believed without a doubt. She trusted in, clung to, relied upon, and committed herself unto the God of Abraham. No one could tell her He wasn't real. No one could sway her from following Him. No one could get her to blaspheme His name, or go against what she knew to be true. She loved God with all her heart and it was seen in her attitude.

True wisdom will grow as we surrender all of our heart, life, and ways to God. Rebekah's life was not her own, it was God's. If we have surrendered our life to God it will be the same; our life is not our own. 1 Corinthians 6:19-20 says, *"Or do you not know that your body is the temple of the Holy Spirit who is in you, whom you have from God, and you are not your own? For you were bought at a price; therefore glorify God in your body and in your spirit, which are God's."* These are just some things to ponder in your heart.

1. Have you truly given your whole life to Christ? _____

2. Does the wisdom of God rule in your life over your emotions? _____

3. Is God glorified in your daily living, in private, and in public? _____

4. What is your attitude toward God? _____

5. Do you let Him correct you and guide you obtaining wisdom when you apply His words?_____

Rebekah's Confidence

6. Rebekah's life was her job. Our life as Christians should be our job for the Lord. Have you surrendered your life as a job for Him? _____

7. In the first four chapters of this book, we see Rebekah physically surrender to God. This process must be done before she could surrender spiritually to Him; which is seen in the last four chapters. Are you in the physical process of surrender? _____

8. What must you do to finish that physical process so that you can surrender spiritually? __
_____
_____

9. What can you learn through the trials you are going through now to bring you closer to God? _____
_____
_____
_____

10. What do you need to give up in your trial to bring you closer to God? _____
_____
_____
_____

11. Are you willing to give up, learn, and finish all that He asks so that you can have a closer relationship with Him? _____
_____
_____
_____

What an amazing woman Rebekah was! She was faithful to God in all that she did. She started her journey with the Lord at the water well giving a drink to a stranger and his livestock. With a servant's heart, she welcomed them into her home and gave them whatever they needed. She made a difficult decision when she left her family to be Isaac's wife. With that decision, she committed to be the best wife to a man she didn't know when she showed him respect and submission. These were all outward evidences of a surrendered heart that could be used even more for God. Now, she is able to go to God for anything, believe He will never lead her wrong, fulfill all that is laid before her and endure to the end with confidence.

www.ingramcontent.com/pod-product-compliance
Lightning Source LLC
Chambersburg PA
CBHW081643040426

42449CB00015B/3443